PENGUIN BOOKS
WRITER'S POSTCARDS

Dipika Mukherjee is an internationally acclaimed writer and sociolinguist with a passion for Southeast Asian literature. With over two decades of experience, she has mentored aspiring writers in the region and founded the prestigious D.K. Dutt Award for Literary Excellence in Malaysia in 2015. Mukherjee has edited five anthologies of Southeast Asian fiction, including the notable titles *Endings and Beginnings* and *Bitter Root Sweet Fruit*.

Her literary achievements include being longlisted for the Man Asian Literary Prize with her debut novel, *Ode to Broken Things*, and winning the UK Virginia Prize for Fiction with her second novel, *Shambala Junction*. She has also authored the captivating short story collection *Rules of Desire* and several poetry collections, such as *Dialect of Distant Harbors* and *The Third Glass of Wine*.

In addition to her writing, Mukherjee is a dedicated educator. She teaches at the Graham School at the University of Chicago and StoryStudio, leveraging her expertise and a PhD in English (Sociolinguistics) from Texas A&M University.

Mukherjee's exceptional work has been recognized through numerous grants and fellowships, including the Esteemed Artist Award from the City of Chicago's Department of Cultural Affairs and Special Events. She has also been honored with prestigious awards like the Quill and Ink Poetry Prize and the Fay Khoo Award for Food+Drink Writing. Through her teaching engagements and creative writing workshops held in various cities worldwide, including Chicago, Amsterdam, New Delhi, Kolkata, Penang, and Kuala Lumpur, she continues to inspire and nurture aspiring writers.

Writer's Postcards

Dipika Mukherjee

PENGUIN BOOKS
An imprint of Penguin Random House

PENGUIN BOOKS

USA | Canada | UK | Ireland | Australia
New Zealand | India | South Africa | China | Southeast Asia

Penguin Books is part of the Penguin Random House group of companies
whose addresses can be found at global.penguinrandomhouse.com

Published by Penguin Random House SEA Pte Ltd
9, Changi South Street 3, Level 08-01,
Singapore 486361

Penguin
Random House
SEA

First published in Penguin Books by Penguin Random House SEA 2023
Copyright © Dipika Mukherjee 2023

ISBN 9789815058772

Typeset in Adobe Caslon Pro by MAP Systems, Bengaluru, India

www.penguin.sg

Contents

Foreword

Solo travel encourages me to stop and wander . . . and craft that experience with words.

It was my mother, after our worst fight, who let me give myself the permission to travel solo. We spat bitterly in Kolkata over something that now feels inconsequential, but at that time, I took umbrage. I, who was supposed to stay on in Kolkata for another week, flew to Varanasi, the closest place I could think of at such short notice.

Of course, I had been on solo trips before, but they were academic conferences in places as far-flung as Lancaster and Cancun and Evora, where lectures on new discoveries in linguistics left little free time before networking over coffee meetings and mayoral receptions. Writing residencies came similarly prearranged, with artist statements outlining the time allocated against the words to be written.

In Benaras, also known as Varanasi or Kashi, for my first accidental solo travel, I checked into a hotel and literally did not know what to do next. And this ancient city, one of the oldest living cities on our planet, unfurled to take in my rage and my grief and my petulance. I came to Varanasi incensed at the pettiness of our mother-daughter quarrel at a time when my father-in-law was seriously ill and a young nephew had been diagnosed with a debilitating disease, but in the morning calm of Varanasi, on a boat ride on the Ganges, the banks erupted in *Achyutam Keshavam*, my father-in-law's favourite religious hymn. Hearing this bhajan being sung by a group of singers at dawn—Benaras has some of the oldest musical gharanas of India—felt like an epiphany, it felt as if I was being told that my father-in-law would survive, as indeed he did, for nine more wonderful years.

Varanasi—in so many ways—taught me to stop and revel in the pleasures of being alone. I stopped at the traditional shakahari restaurants suggested by my rickshaw driver, went into an ancient Shiv shrine next to the Burning Ghats, spoke at length to the artist at a gallery exhibition at the Benaras Hindu University. And I fell in love with this city that had taught generations about death and life and how nothing is ever truly gone.

Now I travel alone at least once a year, allowing myself these mini-residencies such as the one I attended in Redang Island, Malaysia, a few years ago. Sometimes I set out to look for the Dalai Lama and find a community instead. It helps to be able to communicate in English and Bengali and Hindi and Malay—some of the most widely spoken languages of our world—but as Bhutan once taught me, our deepest communications can be through silence and the playfulness of our shared humanity.

As women, we spend so much time nurturing our ties and creating new life, that the life of the mind is often stalled during the child-nurturing years. It feels like freedom to be at an age where I can travel alone, and enjoy the solitude. It is never easy; the ferry ticket seller, the shuttle bus driver, the receptionist, all ask, with a mix of pity and wonder, if I am really travelling alone. Sometimes a question is phrased as, *do you not have any friends?* but then, there is also the kindness of strangers, the solicitude extended to any woman travelling alone.

Of course, I am not the first woman to love my solitude, and as travel becomes safer and more affordable, women all around the world are embarking on journeys alone, in thrilling and adventurous terrain. These words, from a poem originally written by a Mutta—an Indian woman who lived 2,600 years ago—and as translated by Uma Chakravarti and Kumkum Roy, resonate in my heart:

> *So free am I, so gloriously free*
> *Free from three petty things:*
> *From mortar, from pestle, and from my twisted lord*
> *Freed from rebirth and death I am*
> *And all that has held me down*
> *Is hurled away.*[1]

I have a partner of thirty-five years whom I dearly love, but not always while travelling. He is the kind of traveller who wants to see every sight there is to see, to awake at dawn to catch the first burst of light from trek-able hills at sunrise. I prefer to sip from a cup in cafes, taking in the local life as it passes intriguingly by. But together, we explore more, drive just that little bit further . . . we are intrepid.

When my father passed away last year, I was made intensely conscious of how our death rituals require the naming of shaat purush, literally seven fore*fathers*, the mothers obliterated from our memory. We struggled to remember the names of even three women foremothers who had brought my father into being, the original travellers who once moved from their natal homes to strange and foreign places, creating a place for themselves in the feminine infinite we all call home. As American writer Rebecca Solnit points out, 'The ability to tell your own story . . . is already a victory, already a revolt.'

---

[1] 'Mutta', from *Women Writing in India: 600 B.C. to the Present, V: 600 B.C. to the Early Twentieth Century: 1*, ed. by Susie J. Tharu and K. Lalita, p. 68, 1991.

So here is my revolt against historical erasure. The essays are of travel, often solo, sometimes not, but told through a perspective of my own lived experience and imagination, a distinct narrative of a non-white female body as a *flaneuse,* travelling with intention, through our marvellous and varied world.

Saviour

Beacons of Inspiration

'Are you sure you are not a serial killer?'

The Grab driver is joking, of course. He is driving me back to my cottage—Rumah Balai—set within the dense foliage of Rimbun Dahan, where I am the writer-in-residence for five weeks. I have come from my home in Chicago to work on my novel in rural Malaysia, where part of the novel is set.

Tonight is a cloudy night, and the solar lights along the way are completely dark after a few days of rain; there is no illumination at all. Our cottages are not air-conditioned, water is recirculated, and everyone is encouraged to create compost for the herb gardens from the food we consume, but even the eco-warrior in me understands how driving on an untarred road by the light of car headlights can make grown men a little nervous.

During the ride from Kuala Lumpur, we discovered that he has the same last name as a deceased journalist married to my distant uncle in the Bengali community. It never ceases to astonish me that no matter where in the world I am, the enormous Klang Valley operates as a village, and a link to the community can always—always!—be found. We feel like family, and have spent the journey discussing the Grab driver's sixteen-year-old daughter who wants to study creative writing at the Nottingham campus. He worries she will never make money from writing. He is actively dissuading her from her dreams. I have been mentoring Malaysian writers for over two decades, and I know the sad realities of the profession; I have said nothing in her defence.

Suddenly, like a glowing white mirage, Rumah Balai is framed in his headlights. Rumah Uda Manap and Rumah Penang, the two other historical buildings lovingly restored to their former glory, tower like monuments in the darkness. The headlights catch the glints of the flowering trellis in the frosted windowpanes as the light of the moon starts to shine dimly through the clouds.

'Waaaah!' says the driver. 'You *live* here?'

I nod.

'How much is the cost, ah?'

In Asia, I am used to this, to being asked how much something costs, how much my family earns, what I paid for the car now parked in the driveway. There is a genuine curiosity about life, and I learnt very early on to detect if the question is not benign. So now, I tell the driver that I have been awarded a residency, and it costs me nothing.

I open my front door while he waits. His eyes are still open in wonder when he asks if he can see inside.

Much later, I'll think how stupid it is to invite an unknown male inside, no matter how many acquaintances we have in common—I am still a lone woman. But as the lights from the antique lamp holders flood the house, I just open the door wider and invite him in.

The intricately carved four-poster bed with the princess mosquito net, the Chinese cupboard with the frolicking phoenixes, the picturesque kitchen with the enamel mugs . . . he takes it all in.

'I had a Russian passenger once who told me that in Russia, writers are treated like royalty,' he says. He gives me a megawatt grin before he turns to leave. 'I think my daughter should become a writer!'

I stand on the balcony, grinning happily, as much for me as for his daughter, as the red backlights are swallowed into the forest again. One of the many cicaks sounds *thik-thik-thik* over my head. In Bengali, it is saying *truth-truth-truth*.

* * *

Rimbun Dahan is the home of the architect Hijjas Kasturi and his wife, Angela, and is set on fourteen acres, about a half-hour drive from Kuala Lumpur. It is a world of international artists and dancers and painters and sculptors and poets and writers . . . all developing traditional and contemporary art forms. There are multiple artist studios, a dance studio, an air-conditioned artists' lounge, and a library with spotty internet. There is a remarkable underground art gallery. We are free to forage in the extensive herb garden for aloe vera and curry leaves. In a corner of the herb garden, I find the Proiphys amboinensis from the family Amaryllidaceae, which the Malays know as *sepenoh*; not only do the applied leaves reduce swelling, but the plant is also used to fend off the ghostly pontianaks and hantus from entering a new home.

Unfortunately, nothing fends off the mosquitos. Not even the industrial-strength repellent we all have on as we sit poolside during the orientation, where I meet the other residents for the first time. We all slap ourselves periodically.

Angela Hijjas looks at my bare legs and smiles. I have the same indulgent look on my face when Pan, our Belgian Greek horticultural intern, shows up on his first day in shorts. We all learn, rather quickly, that the organic stuff is useless, and it is the industrial-strength DEET-level stuff that is any deterrent.

I meet the other residents—Ruth Marbun, Ajim Juxta, Syarifah Nadhirah, all visual artists—about four days into my residency. During this time, I have tried to figure out the slithery night noises as I awaken from sleep, swept the reptile droppings from kitchen cabinets and floors, and learnt to close my windows so that the resident monkey patriarch wouldn't perch on my windowsill feasting on insects and eyeing me (until I charge at it with my umbrella like a demented Mary Poppins).

Ajim, a Malaysian artist, grew up in rustic surroundings, and Rimbun Dahan does not faze him at all. The Indonesian artist, Ruth, speaks with affection about the large monitor lizards by the pool. Then Nadhirah, or Dee as we call her, tells the story of a family of bats invading her room in the evening, heading straight for the electrical fan and lying, wounded and bleeding, on her floor. Dee called the caretaker, weeping.

I take a swig of my gin and tonic. This is going to be a long five weeks ahead.

* * *

Dee, at twenty-five, is the youngest in the group but insists on walking with me back to Rumah Balai. I, the newbie, have ventured out without a torch or a phone light and planned a trudge in the dark. She and Ajim both walk me back so that no one walks alone. This is the best part of a residency, the bonds that grow and last through the years, because we all create things from the figments of our imagination, things of beauty and courage and conviction which may or may not reach other people . . . and what we do is so inexplicable to the more pragmatic.

With the dry leaves rustling under our feet, Dee asks, hesitantly, whether she can introduce me to her boyfriend, a social activist and writer, who is familiar with my work. As always, this takes me by surprise; in no other country, especially not in the US, where I now live, do I have such name recognition. It is delicious to hand over a credit card for payment in a bookshop in Petaling Jaya and have the cashier gush about a short story. Once a young fan actually did a little jig of joy before taking selfies.

I feel such a close connection to the writing community in Malaysia that although I understand why writers want to be published and known in English-speaking countries—that is certainly where the money is, if at all—I also hope that they speak to the communities they write for. Frequently in my hometown, Chicago, I wonder whether I am the lone Diversity and Inclusion author in an otherwise homogenous panel. The Impostor Syndrome is real for every writer I know, but it has softer edges, and a ductile embrace—at least for me— in Malaysia.

* * *

Two weeks pass by. I wake up to yoga mornings on a balcony shimmering with sunlight sieved through trees. There is the golden glint of spiderwebs, each day a new thread, or one broken, the pattern renewing. The sapling that I anchor my tree pose on starts sprouting pinkish-red shoots at the base as well as on the branch edges.

Kuala Lumpur is still choked with a haze, but here the mornings are fresh and the evenings cleansed by rain.

I get into a pattern of writing through nights, eating at the Warung Selera Ria across the street, and occasional forays into town. Rimbun Dahan is surrounded by a Malay community, traditional in their dressing, and I see no one who looks like me for days. There is a soft, gentle rhythm to the days, and the four resident dogs—Tambi, Betty, Sago, and Susu—occasionally come and sun themselves nearby. I learn to differentiate between the sharp swing of a monkey and the ponderous passage of a monitor lizard. I grow used to the bolt of the striated cicak resident behind the carved fusebox; I stop looking for movements under my pillow at night.

The words come. I publish an article in a newspaper, and have another short story accepted. Shorter pieces flow, but my novel feels like wrestling a crocodile; just when I have quietened the fangs, the tail rears up and whacks me senseless, unable to write another word.

This is my third novel, so I know better than to despair. I am patient in the cyclical rhythms of Rimbun Dahan. I buy a radio because it is too quiet. I tell friends I am writing a Malaysian dystopia by plagiarizing news bulletins.

***

On 16 March, it is Open Day at Rimbun Dahan. Artists are not required to do outreach activities, but I run an ekphrasis workshop to generate writing based on the artwork available at the underground gallery. It is both a challenge and a delight working with Malaysian writers, and for this workshop, I have an Iranian writer and a Syrian poet enrolled.

We start by looking at the whimsical works of Ahmad Fuad Osman, a contemporary Malaysian artist known for his art inspired by social and cultural changes. Like the artist, the writers put themselves into historical Malaya, time-travelling to unpack roots and structures. We all crowd around Australian artist Helen Crawford's *Reflection*; from a distance, the upside-down figure is reminiscent of a lynching, but as you stand around the mirrored bottom, it is the man who is upright, and our images distorted. The participants write furiously about belonging, racism, bullying, inclusivity. Their words are raw and powerful.

Four of the participants—V.S. Lai, Deborah Augustin, Mohammad Amin Kamranimashhadi, Mwaffaq Al-Hajjar—read at Seksan in Bangsar on 30 March, in Malaysia's longest-running monthly reading event curated by Sharon Bakar, an event that has been ongoing for fourteen years. Amin reads from the piece that grew out of the prompt to speak of historical Malaya or a historical homeland; his words take us back to a destroyed Iran:

It's chaos.

I know you always wanted peace and didn't care that much who was ruling this cursed land. 'After all, they are all the same, we are what matter the most.' I remember you telling me this. As disorganized as everything in my life always has been, you always thought that I like these chaotic situations. That this was the reason that I was excited about the street protests and demonstrations. Yes, I wanted a chaotic situation because I hated all the establishments. But there was one routine that I didn't want to lose and that was seeing you in the bookstore.

And now I hate this chaos.

Yes, Rimbun Dahan is inspiring; certainly, the gallery is worth getting lost in for a few hours. It also creates a space where inchoate artistic communities are fostered before they move on to public spheres with confidence and skill.

* * *

Being so close to Kuala Lumpur is both exciting and distracting. I read a Bengali poem by Mallika Sengupta, translated by Amit Mukerjee, at Lit Books for World Poetry Day. The event is organized by Pusaka, and the Creative Director, Pauline Fan, invites fourteen poets to 'The Noise of Time,' an evening of poetry in eleven languages—Malay, English, Bengali, Mandarin, Arabic, Persian, German, French, Spanish, Malayalam, and Russian—with translations into English.

There is the launch for *The Principal Girl: Feminist Tales from Southeast Asia*, a collection of stories from Malaysia and beyond in one beautifully curated collection by Sharifah Aishah Osman and Tutu Dutta.

Commonwealth Writers hosts a panel on the legacy of indenture in contemporary times. It is a thought-provoking panel about erasures and interpretations and ends with a powerful poetry performance by spoken-word poet Melizarani T. Selva, who exceeds all expectations.

A poetry evening in Intunnation is incandescent with the voices of spoken-word poets who use cursed myths of Mahsuri and Gunung Ledang to describe the travails of mothers of LGBTQ children. There is a simultaneous poetry translation from English to Malay. The wordsmiths are bilingual and bidialectal, play with a multiplicity of cultures and the singularity of taboos. They contain multitudes.

Dee and I go to a talk hosted by Sisters in Islam about Muslims and the media. The Q&A session is engaging and electric, sometimes bordering on the forbidden, for too many things are still seditious in the country. Malaysia is exciting for artists for precisely this reason: there are real problems to open dialogues about, the magic realists and the fabulists and the fantasists are coming up with ways to express the forbidden.

Dee, and other Malaysian artists like her, give me hope for a New Malaysia. She is an entrepreneur with her own company but is also engaged in social activism. At Rimbun Dahan, she is an artist, creating a series of exquisite botanic prints to honour our shared ecological legacy.

***

Southeast Asian artists can only stay in Malaysia for a month at a time, so Ruth, the Indonesian artist, leaves first. We go for a farewell lunch at a place where we sit on the floor of raised huts and eat with our hands, drinking coconut water out of small tin pails.

Ruth tells me that what she has found the most inspiring about Rimbun Dahan is the trust implicit in the venue. That this is Angela and Hijjas' home, yet the international artists are instantly made welcome on the grounds, sometimes stumbling upon the couple having a meal, or just strolling in the grounds. The gates are unlocked because the guard dogs are fierce, and we all roam free within the grounds, not as formal guests in someone's home but creative artists free to produce whatever we choose, without being obliged to share it in anyway.

And indeed, Angela is the person I call—because it is her home after all—when I see a rat in my bathroom. She comes at once, with the rat-dispensing dog in tow, the furry Betty who looks more placid than she is. Angela's whistle summons all the dogs, but it is Betty who races into my bathroom, sniffs around the sandalwood soap that the rodent has chewed through, but finds nothing. Lubis, the grounds man who handles dead bats and live rats, is summoned to lay a number of traps.

When I return from a weekend in Kuala Lumpur, they have caught three rats, which are now dead. I am strangely saddened, desolate at the thought of the dead rodents killed in what they also claimed as home, and I am reminded 'Mimesis', a poem by Palestinian-Armenian poet Fady Joudah:

> *If you tear down the web I said*
> *It will simply know*
> *This isn't a place to call home . . .*
> *She said that's how others*
> *Become refugees isn't it?*

I am the intruder in Rimbun Dahan, within a habitat that will continue long after I am gone. It teaches me empathy when a young wild boar circumambulates the house looking for an open gate to get out. I back away slowly when it pauses some eight feet away, staring at me. It squeals in distress; it has no tusks and looks like a young one separated from the pack. Angela and I sit on the balcony sipping tea and watching him lope around, then she gets up and opens the gates, which are usually locked, so that he can find multiple exits.

Ruby Subramaniam, a visual artist who stayed at Balai Rumah during her artistic residency in 2018, asks me whether I have felt the magic of this place. To her, the ground seemed so hallowed that she took long walks by the light of the moon, communing with all the living creatures around her.

***

So how did Rimbun Dahan begin?

Tun Dr Mahathir Mohamed was the prime minister when the idea of Rimbun Dahan as an artists' residency first started to germinate; the Australian prime minister had called Dr Mahathir 'recalcitrant', and the relationship between Australia and Malaysia was especially fraught. The Kasturis had strong connections to both countries and figured that an artistic bridge could help in healing the political rift. An artistic exchange was initiated between Australian visual artists and Malaysian counterparts, which, over the past twenty years, has developed into a programme that encompasses creative aspirants from all over the world.

What the Kasturis have created is a shining beacon in a country where funding for the arts is absent or racially divisive.

***

The Grab car drivers all know the legendary architect of Malaysia Hijjas Kasturi, but they talk far more about Bilqis, his daughter. In 2015, Bilqis dropped protest-yellow balloons containing the words 'democracy', 'free media', and 'justice' into a function attended by the then prime minister, Datuk Seri Najib Tun Razak.

'Bilqis is like a hero. You know, like that Tiananmen Square, that fellow that stood in front of the tank?'

He sees my disbelief in the rearview mirror.

'Okay lah, maybe not on the same, but you know what I mean . . . we all talk-talk only, but she *did* something.'

I finally meet Bilqis when she pulls up to Rimbun Dahan in an unapologetically bright yellow car. We chat briefly, about dance and writing and Rimbun Dahan. I will leave this art sanctuary in a few days, but I feel assured that the legacy of Rimbun Dahan will live on for years to come, allowing many more artists to create and affecting our communities in many subtle ways. This place will continue feeding the soul of this nation.

There is a new gamelan troupe that is setting up its equipment now. The two master craftspeople from Bali tap at the instruments to tune them, while the group from Kuala Lumpur watches and learns. *Tap-tap*. A bird chirps in response. The melody melds into the breeze.

To Keep My Brother Alive, I Will Fly 7,500 Miles for Diwali

In Bengal, two days after Diwali is Bhai Phota. On this day Bengali sisters become Jamuna, the sister of Jomdoot the God of Death, reigning over mortality. We place a holy mark on our brother's forehead, and our mantras go like this:

> *Bhaier kapale dilam phota,*
> *Jamuna dae Jomke phota,*
> *Ami di amar bhaike phota,*
> *Jom duare porlo kaanta*
>
> *I put a phota on my brother's forehead,*
> *Just as Yamuna did for Jamdoot,*
> *I give a phota to my brother*
> *and bar the door to death.*

Amit has always been my protective big brother—older by eight years—aware of distress I did not always have the voice to articulate. In 2016, when the phone rang on a Saturday night in Chicago, which is Sunday in Delhi and the time when family usually calls, I was unprepared.

> *Amit was in a cycling accident . . .*
> *He is in a coma . . .*

There is the possibility of a severe brain injury . . .
No one knows whether he will survive . . .

I reach the hospital after flying 7,500 miles from Chicago, changing planes in Delhi, and reaching Kanpur past midnight. At the ICU, Amit looks asleep. He is less damaged than I had braced myself for, and despite the wires and tubes, he looks as if he could wake up any time. I hold his arm tentatively, afraid to hurt him, but there is no reaction at all.

I look over the notes on the brain damage, a broken rib, leg fracture. There is a broken collarbone injury so severe, that the doctors press on it to assess the immediate flinch; pain is Amit's only connection to a reactive brain.

I cannot watch this necessary pinching and prodding, and turn away. I want to shout at the doctors to stop hurting my brother, but I am silent as they measure the degree of movement, notice the heightened angle of wince, then lean in to see the pupils' minuscule dilation.

For the first time, I wonder about the stupidity of bartering with Gods.

* * *

Amitabha is a common name, signifying the Buddha of Immeasurable Light and Life. Amit was born in Buddhist Bangkok.

At the news of Amit's coma, I had rushed to my altar in Chicago, lit sandalwood incense in the dark, then switched on the prayer lamp of many Buddhas carved into stone.

The electric bulb briefly sputtered. Then died.

I found a new bulb, an energy saver supposed to work for years. Nothing. There was no light. Increasingly frantic, I looked for another bulb, then another, maniacally tearing apart packaging. opening wires, tightening tiny screws, checking a fuse, aligning frayed rubber and metal . . . and stars.

Still the light would not switch on. On the twenty-fourth of January a bus hit my brother and it was still the twenty-fourth in the United States, and I wanted to turn this into a bad dream I could wake from, summoning my inner Didion into magical thinking.

The darkness was resolute. Six Buddhas on each side, four sides. Twenty-four. I had a flight to catch in a few hours. Before that, a universe to bend.

The poet Iqbal wrote:

> *Khudi ko kar buland itna ke har taqdeer se pehle,*
> *Khuda bande se khud pooche, bata, teri raza kya hai?*
> *Sharpen your will till so unyielding, so determined,*
> *that even Gods must ask at each fork of destiny, what is*
> ***your** desire?*

There was a bedside lamp in the guest bedroom, with a flat base. On this, I placed an ox-bone Buddha, a souvenir from Bhutan. I slammed on the altar my wrathful offering, praying: Return Amit to us . . . Make him wake up!

This light switched on, and a glow suffused the golden Buddha face, benevolent Amitabha's right hand in *bhumisparshamudra,* rooted to earth, turning anger to wisdom, indulgent of human hubris.

And there was this certainty in my heart, that no matter how long the route to India, no matter how many flight changes to get there, I would reach in time. Amit would live.

My brilliant, amazing, genius of a brother—even with a traumatic brain injury—would live.

At the hospital in Kanpur, I wondered for the first time: Would he have wanted this?

* * *

I was sixteen when Amit had—for the first and last time—slapped me across my face.

I am the darling of my family, the only girl born after two older brothers. I remember looking at the flame of the forest tree, the krishnachura blooming into fiery blossoms against green branches, the colours merging as my eyes watered.

Amit had been quizzing me on complex math equations so that I would pass my tenth-grade board exams in Delhi. My father's diplomatic career had taken us all over the world but international schools had unprepared me for the gruelling math of the Indian system; I was very likely to fail and have to repeat that entire academic year. But I was a teenager in love with the bad boy from my class, and all I could concentrate on was how late I would be for a date.

The slap was so quick that I later wondered if it had been an effort to physically turn my head to my books, a movement stronger than my brother had actually intended. Amit looked shocked. There is no apology necessary when discipline is enforced from an elder to the younger, so we cut the math tutorial short, and my brother drove me to my date on his Royal Enfield motorbike.

Amit continued to tutor me in math and I passed that subject with distinction; the highest grade possible. My brother would go on to change the trajectory of my life in significant ways: When I applied for graduate studies in the US at the same university where he taught Computer Science, my letters

of acceptance and of financial aid would be CC'd to him from
the department; When I wanted to marry a man from another
caste and my father refused to accept a son-in-law who could
not be seated at religious ceremonies with kin, it was Amit
who argued—successfully—that the problem was not with my
choice, but the antiquated socio-religious framework my family
still upheld.

* * *

I grew up on *Thakumar Jhuli*—that wildly popular collection
of Bengali folklore by Dakshinaranjan Mitra Majumdar,
published in 1907.

I learnt, at the lap of oral storytellers, that sibling love is a
superpower. I believed girls can save brothers by a force of will.

In the story of the three royal siblings—Arun, Barun, and
Kiranmala—the siblings lived in the forest after their mother
was banished from the kingdom by the King. They built a most
magnificent fortress to live in, and one day, a holy man visited
their palace and told them about the hill of Maya, filled with
the treasures of a tree of diamond with golden fruit, a golden
talking bird, and the elixir of water from a magical spring.

Tempted by the treasures, Arun set off on a journey, leaving
behind his dagger for his younger siblings, saying, 'If there is
ever rust on this blade, know I am in danger.'

The day the siblings found rust on the dagger, Barun
immediately set out on the same journey in search of his
brother. He gave his sister a silver bow and arrow, warning, 'If
these weapons are tarnished, know I am in danger.'

The days passed, and one day, Kiranmala saw the bow
and arrow transformed into dull grey from its silver shine.
She immediately took her sword and stepped out to save her

brothers, walking faster than the wind to reach the magical hill. Voices cried out, 'Oh look back, look at us, once!' But she didn't turn to see the source of the noise. The voices screeched, 'STOP, or you will die!' Kiranmala remained steadfast and walked on until she reached her destination.

When she found the treasures, the talking bird instructed her to take a branch of the diamond tree, and sprinkle the water on the rocks. The rocks miraculously transformed into people— including her two brothers petrified into stone.

She brought them all back into consciousness.

* * *

We do not need to lose someone to grieve. Pauline Boss describes ambiguous loss as a state of fluctuating between hope and hopelessness; when someone dies, there are clear rituals to mark a passing, but when a loved one is alive but lost to us, there is no closure.

Pray for a miracle, Amit's neurosurgeon advised. Amit's brain scan looked like that of Michael Schumacher's, the most famous traumatic brain injury of our times; when the German race-car driver was in a skiing accident in 2013, it derailed his promising career and he remains under medical supervision at his home.

My father asks: Why do we think we are exempt from disaster? That bad things that happen, cannot happen to us?

My father—at ninety-four—has lost his parents, and all seven siblings. He is the last one still alive to remember the colour of eight types of village spinach, the slime of river-mud in his toes, the taste of sweet-river fish captured in hand-woven baskets; he remembers days of a full home, unsevered communities, an unpartitioned homeland.

What is it, that makes us so special, to be exempt from life?

My father is determined to live until Amit recovers. He gives me the wisdom of the Upanishads, words written in the sixth century BC:

> *You are what your deep, driving desire is.*
> *As your desire is, so is your will*
> *As your will is, so is your deed*
> *As your deed is, so is your destiny*

* * *

Every year, since Amit's accident in 2016, I have been going back to India for Bhai Phota. Those of us living in one of the many-tentacled diasporas of this global age—the Chinese, the Indian, the Filipino, the Nigerian—understand exactly what Mohsin Hamid meant when he wrote in *Exit West*: '. . . for when we migrate, we murder from our lives those we leave behind.'

I refuse to murder my brother from my life. So, I take a COVID test ninety-six hours before my flight from Chicago, then quarantine in Delhi for the two weeks before 16 November, which is when Bhai Phota falls in 2020.

There is always hope. My brother's accident changed so many lives, reverberating in mine much harder than that single slap that changed my academic trajectory so many years ago. Last time I was with my brother, reading to him, I read out loud these words by Mary Oliver:

> *Someone I loved once gave me*
> *a box full of darkness.*
>
> *It took me years to understand*
> *that this, too, was a gift.*

Hope and Mangroves

The Redang air is electric during the monsoon season. Breezes rustle through palm trees and the air swirls into a fog before bursting through the sky with a welcome breath of cool on this tropical island in Malaysia. It is November, off-peak season and a strange time to visit a resort town. Bad weather has suspended travel, and on my first night here I am the only guest. There is no public transportation on the island, and Malay farming families make up most of the permanent population. On walks, I meet more roving monitor lizards than people. I share my meals with nearby chattering monkeys. But I am here to grieve a family tragedy and to work on a manuscript that feels both cathartic and impossible to finish. The solitude suits me.

One day, another deluge begins just as I reach a tiny lunch shack overlooking the frothing sea. The thatched roof is so leaky I am seated with two strangers at the only table safe from the invading rain. One of them is Hashimi Ismail, and he wears a fluorescent shirt and a luminous smile. Over the din of pouring rain, he tells me he is in Redang to lead a group of students in a replanting effort to restore the coastal mangrove forests decimated by rapid tourism, including the creation of a new airport runway. The mangrove communities on the island's northern coast provide important habitat for numerous species, including the endangered green and critically endangered hawksbill sea turtles, and this habitat destruction has Malaysian scientists and global environmental activists concerned. Hashimi has been involved in local restoration work for over a decade and invites me to visit one of their nursery sites.

I always try to say *yes* to the serendipity of new roads opening up during my travel as a solo woman, clearly brown, no longer very young. Strangers open up homes, offer food, and even unsolicited advice can be welcome.

So the next evening, I join Hashimi's group, a gaggle of about thirty ten-to-twelve-year-olds and a handful of teachers gathered around some beached boats. Despite the humid heat, everyone is covered from head to toe, socks on feet, hats on heads, and even their necks protected by scarves. I quickly understand why when a mass of mosquitoes descends to feast on my uncovered skin. Everyone is dressed for the bugs and mud and prickly branches, and I feel like the idiot from Chicago in my shorts and open-toed sandals.

The children jostle and tease one another as we trek along a narrow path towards the first nursery site. Their excitement is palpable. As Hashimi calls out the various plant life surrounding us, a hush comes over the boisterous group. He points to the *buta-buta* oozing a milky latex that can cause temporary blindness, the smooth-barked *tumu merah* with narrow elliptic leaves, and the *teruntum merah* with fragrant tubular red flowers. The children repeat the names in Malay; one asks a question about the *putat laut* seeds, which can be ground into powder to stun or kill fish for easy catching. I nearly stumble over a *mengkuang laut* fruit—part pineapple, part grenade—as the conversation turns to mangroves.

Mangroves have a unique reproductive strategy in the plant world, Hashimi tells us. Most flowering plants release dormant seeds, but mangroves are viviparous, meaning their seeds, or propagules, begin to germinate and develop while still attached to the parent tree. When a propagule detaches from its parent, it continues to develop as it floats in the water, eventually sprouting roots and leaves if it finds a suitable habitat.

We arrive at an open marshy area where previously gathered mangrove propagules are heaped on to the sand like bundles of green cigars. The students flock around, examining the samples. At first, they are shy with me, the only stranger. When I ask how you can tell if a propagule is ready for planting, Marsya just covers her face with her hands and giggles before Mohammad grabs a handful and points to little roots and tiny emergent leaves. When I carefully pick out just one sample from his hand, he patiently schools me. 'You must take six,' he urges, holding out the entire bunch in his hand, 'not just one.' They won't all survive the transplantation, so there is safety in numbers. Together we crouch next to Nur as she manoeuvres propagules into the swampy ground. All the girls wear traditional *tudung* head coverings in various colours, and many of the boys don hats or wear bandannas wrapped around their foreheads. They hunker on the ground together, a sea of colour bobbing above the soil. Beyond them, a forest of mature mangroves rises, verdant leaves reflected in the water, a small soaring in the distance.

The children are good mentors. They have travelled far by boat to come here from their rural primary schools in the coastal state of Terengganu. For them, Redang is a big town full of new experiences. But they seem at home in the forest, laughing and ribbing one another when one plants a seedling badly. Their enthusiasm and stamina are contagious, and I imagine them making this country bloom for generations to come. Already the neighbouring restoration sites with more mature transplants form a growing curtain along the airport's fenced boundary. I am tired and sweaty, my hands are wet and muddy, and my knees creak from so much bending, but it feels like the evening melts into the night too soon.

A Journey to the Dalai Lama

It was January 2013, when I first set out to meet the Dalai Lama. His Holiness lives in exile in India, in McLeodganj, a city in the clouds where the Buddhist chants are as clear as the calls of the Himalayan bulbul. It is a retreat in the perfect sense, and I had just started to write my third novel, a novel I felt compelled to write because a monk who was about to immolate himself had started talking inside my head.

I had left home two weeks earlier for a series of literary festivals in India—starting with Hyderabad and ending with Delhi. I didn't really have a plan for McLeodganj. I had visited Tibet in 2011, and the changing face of Lhasa, where the culture of the Chinese Han people seemed to be wiping out the native Tibetans, had been disturbing. The road signs in Tibet are now inscribed with the rigid straight lines and flailing arms of the pinyin, overshadowing the gentle curlicues of the Tibetan alphabet flowing around the prayer bells and circling mandalas. Soon after this trip to Tibet, a Tibetan monk on the verge of self-immolation started talking in my head, incessantly, and as most writers know only too well, the only way you can silence such a voice is by writing the words down.

But I had also lived and worked in Shanghai for almost three years, mingling with intelligent and humane Chinese academics and writers and students; I could not write an un-nuanced morality tale of good vs evil about Tibet. As an

Indian, I knew we had our own Sikkim and Kashmir, contested lands that are considered by many of the local people to be occupied states taken by the behemoth Indian Government. So I was headed for McLeodganj in 2013 to make sense of this, to find a monk like the one talking in my head. A well-connected official in New Delhi had liked my debut novel, then became interested in my subsequent work, and offered to help with research. Over lunch at a fancy Indo-Chinese restaurant in South Delhi, she had casually asked, 'Since you are going to McLeodganj, would you like to see the Dalai Lama?'

Was that even a rhetorical question?

I left Delhi armed with the telephone numbers of the Dalai Lama's chief translator and the Director of the Tibetan Archives. The Dhauladhar Range came into view in the early morning of my bus ride from Delhi, lighting up the sky with its snowy cape and erasing the darkness with a warm milky glow. First, there was one white peak, then another and another, until at every turn the view dazzled even more. Such pure whiteness as I have never seen, against the soft twinkle of the night sky, and the valley glowed with a faint light below.

It seemed like an excellent omen; I assumed I would just get into McLeodganj, find my monk, engage him in conversation, meet the Dalai Lama, and be on my way. Nothing to it. Eleven days, mission accomplished. Then I could get back to my real life, the routine of poring over books, making sense of this experience, and putting it into a novel. I reached McLeodganj, checked into the exuberantly painted Pink House, ordered some ginger honey tea and waited for the universe to deliver.

Which it quickly did. The Dalai Lama's translator returned my call to say that His Holiness was on a retreat and would be seeing no one in the next two weeks. He would be happy to talk to me, but bad timing, maybe His Holiness would be available the next time? The proprietor of the Pink House asked if I knew that there was a waiting line for *years* to see His Holiness and that I needed to apply online. The guy at the local pharmacy told me Tibetans wait all their lives, but alas, most die before they are able to see His Holiness.

I felt like a complete idiot. All the old insecurities, that maybe I was a writer who had stumbled into this calling with no idea of what I was doing, came rushing back. I was in the wrong profession, and clearly too stupid for this.

As I walked along the empty roads of McLeodganj in low season I felt completely wretched. The Tibetan volunteer associations were closed until the summer crowds returned and I had no idea where to even begin looking for my monk. It was biting cold after a slight grey drizzle and I was wearing boots.

Suddenly a man offered to shine my dusty boots for a low price—*Business was so bad nowadays Didi*, he called out to me in Hindi. He had come all the way from Rajasthan but there was no work now. I stopped at his stand and started taking off my boots. As I bent down, I could see, behind the man, a green sign waving in the wind just below street level: 'English Conversation Teachers Wanted'. It was the headquarters of the Ex-Political Prisoners of Tibet.

I couldn't wait. I told the Rajasthani man I'd be right back and ducked into the low doorway in my socks, following the signs to the 'Office'. The lone man sitting there spoke halting English and no Hindi. He had to dial someone else. I waited below the pictures of Mahatma Gandhi and the Dalai Lama. And I waited. And I waited. Finally, I wandered around the building, looking at pictures of the ways in which political prisoners are tortured. There were paintings of tiny thumb-cuffs used to string up men, and women with fish hooks in their vaginas. There was a list of the martyred, most of whom had barely begun their adult lives.

When I had waited for thirty-five minutes and was about to give up a very dishevelled man called me in. Initially sceptical about why I was at their office, he warmed up after googling my university affiliations while I silently waited again. 'Tomorrow,' he said, 'you can begin to teach Conversational English.'

Over the next ten days, I taught a group of men and women who were all ex-political prisoners and had fled from Tibet. In my class of nine, five were monks, four were not (although one among them used to be). I was their English conversation partner and so they told me about escaping on foot from Tibet, walking over the Himalayan ranges with inadequate footwear, trying to avoid the splitting ice and the strong currents on streams. When there were children, they took turns to piggyback the young ones, but inevitably, they lost some. They talked about walking through the moonlit fog-shaded mountain passes and sleeping through the warmer days. Some were lost in these passes, while the sick had to be abandoned. They were crippled by homesickness and hunger and exhaustion but always hounded by the fear of Chinese bullets.

Every day, from 4.30 to 6.00 in the evening, I heard their stories. Then I went to a meditation class to distance my mind from so much human misery. In the mornings I would go to the Tibetan archives, where the Director opened up the ancient Buddhist texts, the *Jataka Tales*, that say much about the fortitude of the Tibetan people. There were beautiful murals everywhere, describing the cycle of life. Other mornings I would go to the Dalai Lama's Temple to speak to the chief translator. I wrote every day—a well of words sprouted, bursting to be free, but they were not my words; they were the stories of the Tibetans I met going about their business in every street corner.

I didn't meet the Dalai Lama. Instead, McLeodganj taught me much about serendipity, and trusting the universe. About ceding control and slowing down. The day before I was about to leave, the lights went out after a relentless storm. My first reaction was, *Why doesn't India ever get any better?* but I was forced, in the dim light, to watch the strong winds lashing the trees, which seemed to reach out to each other. The conifers and the shrubbery, all shivering leaves in a dance of solidarity against the elements. Then a flock of kites came. At first, I thought they were in distress, wheeling in the wind with raucous cries, but then it was clear that they were riding the wind, as confident surfers ride the crest. And meanwhile, the mountains in the background were being slowly dusted with a cloud of white, like a divine hand sprinkling powdered sugar on chocolate.

I had lived through monsoon storms in the Klang Valley in Malaysia, but glued to a TV or a computer screen, I usually missed Nature in her glory. McLeodganj held up this spirit of beauty in its entire splendour, in nature as well as in the hearts of the indomitable and compassionate Tibetan people. I had thought that this journey would be about meeting the Dalai Lama, but it turned out to be a larger connection with ordinary Tibetans, whose stories needed to be told.

'Maybe you'll meet the Dalai Lama after your book is published,' said the Director of the Library, 'One person blows up a building and the media has pictures everywhere, but our youth are burning themselves and no one cares. Please tell their story.'

* * *

On 4 September 2015, two and a half years after I had first set out on my quest, I met His Holiness the Dalai Lama. By then, I had started to tell the Tibetan stories, and McLeodganj continued to call me, and finally, I received an audience with His Holiness.

I had read about his congeniality, but I was unprepared for the favourite uncle vibe he exuded, putting an easy arm around my shoulder for photographs, his eyes always curious, always kind. He quizzed me about my teaching experience in Shanghai and about the book I was writing, as if we had all the time in the world, although there was a line waiting to meet him.

I murmured some platitudes about how proud I was that he was living in India now, and he must speak Hindi fluently by now, whereas alas, my Mandarin Chinese was rudimentary at best.

He had a twinkle in his eye. 'Let's do this,' he suggested, 'I ask you a question in Hindi, and you reply to me in Mandarin Chinese. Shall we?'

We both laughed uproariously at how badly I'd lose at his game and then said our goodbyes.

McLeodganj, in the first journey of eleven days, had already taught me the truism of the old cliché—it is the journey; it is ALL about the journey. We all have the same destination in the end, no matter what lives we live, but sometimes, along the journey, we are touched by Grace, if we are lucky to live at a time when great souls still walk the earth.

Calligraphic Lives in China and Tibet

There are many kinds of freedom in our world. Ultimately, we all have to make a personal decision about what we are willing to live with, and what we choose to ignore.

> *Shoes, wet from yesterday's rain, squelch*
> *in reluctance. The teenager trips down stairs*
> *black hair, black Man U shirt, black shorts.*
> *Woohooh, he sings, let's go dudelums!*
> *his voice full of a Shanghai adventure.*
>
> *I am not so sure. I miss the writers*
> *at the Mezrab, words framed by gentle*
> *clanks of trams of Amsterdam*
> *Iranian bread, black tea, arguing*
> *about art and artifice.*
>
> *Here, a silent smog overpowers—*
> *food broiling and boiling, warm steamy*
> *smoke of stews and preserved vegetables—*
> *in the French Concession seeking*
> *a shared history, there's only fog.*

In late 2009, we moved from Amsterdam to Shanghai. I faced the prospect of being a trailing spouse for the second time in my life; our move to Texas in 1989 was precipitated by my acceptance into a doctoral programme, and the move to Singapore in 1999 was after I was offered an expatriate position with Nanyang Technological University. In both cases, my husband had followed after six months. Amsterdam had been my first experience with the trailing-spouse-syndrome, and it had been difficult to find an academic position which paid a regular salary.

My writing network of American expatriates in Amsterdam was the most astonished by the decision to move to Shanghai. *But why?* a writer wailed. *You will have no freedom.* Another colleague declined a move to China because—*horrors!*—their almost-adult-teenager could end up marrying a Chinese girl. There are many ways to express racism in post-colonial expatriation.

A life of expatriation allows one to see the failure of the nation-state in various permutations from up close. No country is perfect, and one can only hope that the next one will be flawed in ways easier to accept.

Shanghai was large and brash and pulsating in a way that reminded me of Mumbai; another Asian megapolis. It had the same frenetic pace: mad traffic jams and food shops open day and night, cars revving up at pedestrian walkways whether people were still crossing or not, and office goers stabbing elevator doors shut because they were late for meetings.

There was an incivility about daily life. The Dutch are among the happiest people on Earth, certainly their children are declared so in many studies, and our stay in the Netherlands allowed for walks in the rain and long bike rides and days for self-care. In Shanghai, everyone was running late for a train that was leaving the station—a superfast bullet train with few stops. The pollution index readings were so high, that walking for leisure was a terrible idea.

And in this milieu, while my husband quickly climbed up a career ladder, I was searching for an identity beyond that of a trailing spouse. We had moved into a gated community and had a housekeeper and a driver and my lifestyle had grown both extravagant and shallow. Then, a few months later, in a process that seemed extremely opaque, I was offered the position of Distinguished Professor (211 Professorship) at Shanghai International Studies University (SISU).

This job came at a time when I was questioning my life choices; during our move from Amsterdam to Shanghai, when I had been applying for many jobs, I was offered a VP position with Deloitte. It was a tempting offer but would split our family into two. It would offer me a meaningful job in Hyderabad, India, with perks that included the coverage of medical treatments for my ageing parents in India. I declined as my youngest son had two years left of high school (my older child was away in college in the US), and it seemed untenable to split the family when we had managed to co-parent the children through stints in Texas, Malaysia, Singapore, Ohio, Amsterdam, and now Shanghai.

But when men are expatriated and their wives follow, it can be a lonely life, shorn of the validation which had energized me before. When the call came in Shanghai to accept the Distinguished Professorship, I had just come out of the shower on another slow day, and was wandering around barefoot when I picked up the phone. My first instinct was to insist, *no*, I could not rush to their campus at such short notice, I was so used to my slower pace.

My last—and only—interview on campus had been peremptory: I had rushed to the campus expecting to meet the Head of Linguistics and some colleagues, but was ushered to a lofty room with four long tables joint into a square. The sumptuous surroundings made the room more a palatial dining room from Versailles than an academic interview space, and seated at the head of the table was the University President. He was flanked by male heads of departments and administrative staff. There were two women present, one of whom was the Head of Linguistics, a scholar with whom I had corresponded by email for weeks.

There were two people being interviewed that day; besides me, there was an American professor who had taught at SISU for almost a decade already, and he was seeking a promotion. I needed a translator, which mercifully slowed my interview down, so that I was able to locate a thumb drive with some research papers and presentation slides which illustrated my research interests and publication history. It was not the most bizarre interview I have ever been subjected to—once, for a position at an International Islamic University in Malaysia I had been quizzed by a panel of seven men about why I agreed women should cover their hair—but here, in China, there was incomprehensible talk all around me, the questioning coming from all directions, with no roadmap to where this was leading. I had no idea I would get the job, and I fully expected not to.

But there it was, and when I answered the call, an administrative assistant from Human Resources was asking me to get to SISU *now* so that I could accept a position to teach at the University.

'No,' I said. 'I'm not free today.'

A few minutes later, it was the Department Chair, urging me to make a short appearance. It was Women's Day, and they wanted to appoint me with some fanfare on this exact day, no it could not wait until tomorrow.

Immediately, the spectre of the Imposter Syndrome reared its ugly head. Was I being employed only because they needed to hire a woman? I deliberately tamped down my outrage as I reflected on the long email correspondence with the Department Head, and the qualifications and publications that had led me to even apply for the position. The other person being honoured today was the American professor who had interviewed with me, a Man. I, clearly, was being ridiculously petty about this.

When I reached the University, it was like a prize-giving ceremony, with huge yellow banners proclaiming messages I could not read, and photographers taking pictures of the American professor and me being awarded our papers, individually, then jointly, then with the University President, then with a phalanx of academics I did not know at all.

I smiled through it all, taking my cue from the other professor who beamed with genuine delight.

I was now a Distinguished Professor at the Department of Linguistics at SISU. From March 2010 to August 2012, I would supervise graduate students and teach postgraduate courses in Applied Linguistics from March 2010 to August 2012, returning to China to finish my contract even after my family relocated to Chicago in August 2011.

* * *

In an alleyway a man grabs a woman
spinning her around as she claws
flings her on the pavement; she lies
there, not bleeding, taking short choked
breaths of air. No one stops.
He tries to jerk her to her feet
she hits his groin with a stiletto.

I am haunted by inner reels which
refuse deletion. Random violence
in too-shared spaces, jostling
through life in teeming crowds . . .
I know this too well.

I start investigating the robustness of the Shanghai dialect, with a group of researchers. After a series of modifications to the language policy, the relationship between Putonghua and other regional dialects is defined as complementary in contemporary China. Putonghua, the standard variety of Mandarin Chinese, meaning 'common language', has been the national language of the People's Republic of China (PRC) ever since the Chinese Communist Party (CCP) came to power in 1949 and the wording of the paper we begin to write is cagey, for the 'complementary' situation of the dialects and Putonghua is premised on the fact that Putonghua is largely used in public domains whereas the dialects are largely used in private domains. However, as Putonghua started to enter private domains freely and become the family language, the survival of the Shanghai dialect was in jeopardy.

What piqued my research interest in Shanghai was the question of language maintenance, especially the thriving Shanghai dialect, despite the official roadblocks. By 2010, after five decades of Putonghua promotion ranging over generations of school education, Putonghua had spread to every part of Chinese social life, and sometimes became the family language used in daily life, replacing ancestral dialects. Putonghua was the language of education, government and mass media. It was also the financially powerful language, of commerce, in business, transportation and tourism in most cities and villages.

My sociolinguistic research interests have focused on migrant discourses (especially language shifts in diasporic Indian communities) as well as variation in multilingual societies with complex language planning issues. In my work with Malaysian-Bengali women in the Klang Valley in Malaysia and the Suriname-Hindustani community in Amsterdam, I have documented the robustness of language maintenance in minority communities despite the language being under threat from more economically viable and higher-status languages in the repertoire of speakers.

Putonghua, without a doubt, was the hardest language I have ever undertaken to learn as an adult; I just could not hear the differences, and tones eluded me completely. I tried learning the language with my fifteen-year-old son who had brought me to Shanghai instead of fleeing to Hyderabad in the first few months, and his growing fluency was enviably effortless, while mine remained an embarrassment.

At SISU, as I worked on documenting the current state of the Shanghai dialect as it is being used in Shanghai, especially in the media, the duality of language expansion and language survival in China's fast-growing economic capital became of interest to linguists, for language resilience can also be a form of resistance. But also, at the university, I was embarrassing myself with my inability to distinguish between Professor Xu and Professor Shu when they came up in conversations, as the names were homonyms to me, but distinct to my colleagues.

I had to keep reminding myself that no language is inherently more difficult than any other, for any child, in any part of the world, can string together meaningful sentences by the age of three. Languages are more difficult to learn as one gets older, but there are exceptions, and a multiligual like me, who speaks three languages or more, were supposed to have an advantage.

Nothing worked.

I deferred to my colleagues in the data collection, but worked on developing publishable journal papers with them. I developed a deep respect for my graduate students, young men and women who taped my lectures in English, and then transcribed, with a dictionary in hand as required. I learnt humility while being the expert in disseminating knowledge in academic classrooms.

My first academic job was at Nanyang Technological University in Singapore, where, as a very green Assistant Professor, I was gently reminded, that despite my newly-minted American doctorate, I could do little to get students to challenge me in classroom discussions in the way American students are conditioned to do from elementary school. Years of a Confucian respect for hierarchy and deep veneration for educators made my Singaporean students unwilling to argue with me, or even speak up, in class.

The Shanghai campus was European in design, and I taught in freshly constructed Grecian buildings set among fountains and lakes, as the students offered Westernized names like Jack and Anna. However, the lack of opinions on language change in the face of an official language policy was distinctly Chinese.

The official stance had been steady, vacillating between a strong promotion of Putonghua versus a more benign allowance for polyglotism. Language policy in the 1950s had as its goal the spread of Putonghua in every domain of social life and for China to become a monolingual society, and the emphasis had been on rapid growth and ideological purity. However, the problems with the implementation of the one-language policy were many, ranging from mistranslations to active resistance to Putonghua. During the Great Leap Forward, launched in 1958, and its aftermath, tolerance of ethnic diversity diminished drastically.

I sometimes felt like my class and I were under surveillance. It would take two semesters to break through the silence of students and have meaningful dialogues in class. As a way to break through the quiet, I organized an exchange with Shanghai migrant schools through Stepping Stones, a volunteer English teaching organization in Shanghai. My students visited migrant schools in various districts—including Minhang, Songjian and Pudong—to converse in English with migrant communities from around China.

To open them up to the world, they were encouraged to write research papers for presentation at conferences in Australia, the USA, the Philippines, and Malaysia. Three years after I left China, I would meet one of my students in Leiden, the Netherlands, where she was pursuing a PhD. I couldn't have been prouder.

* * *

> *Every morning, the river choked*
> *by a lush hyacinth carpet of green is*
> *pierced by the fishermen making themselves*
> *small in narrow barricades, squatting*
> *on haunches, fishing in silence.*
>
> *A river, food, friends and time.*
> *We glamorize lives beyond this gated*
> *community, feel a bend in the river as*
> *our lost opportunity . . . which it—*
> *clearly—is not.*

My life in Shanghai was like living in a parallel, unreal universe. We had a live-in housekeeper and a full-time driver and our lives in the gated communities of expatriates were more luxurious than what we were used to. Trailing spouses, usually wives, became tai-tais—wealthy women with deep pockets and much leisure, women who lunched frequently at places on the Bund in high-end restaurants as expensive as those in Chicago or New York.

The owner of one of the iconic Bund restaurants, M on the Bund, also ran the Shanghai Literary Festival every year, an ostentatious gala that brought the literary talent of the world to Shanghai. The clientele was not always literary at these events, for the cost of entry, and any event with a meal, was beyond what struggling writers or students could afford. During my first year in Shanghai, a friend was launching her new novel; along with the heartfelt congratulations on the social media post, one person regretted not being able to make it to the event as she had a nail appointment which clashed with the book launch, and as she was flying to the Maldives on vacation, the beauty salon could not be cancelled at any cost.

I took nine SISU students to hear a bestselling American linguist, Deborah Fallow, talk about her book *Dreaming in Chinese* at the Glamour Bar inside M On the Bund. It was a lunch event, and as the cost for lunch was about twenty times higher than what the students and I paid for our delicious lunches at the many canteens around SISU, and as the university would cover only the cost of the tickets for the students, we opted for the talk only, no meal included. The students were asked to sit on windowsills as chairs were hurriedly procured for them; as if they were interlopers. Around us, the gentle clink of silverware on fine china continued unabated. The students huddled among themselves, seemingly unperturbed by the rudeness of the festival staff, and even asked thoughtful questions at the Q&A after the event.

I bristled at the whole experience. There is a persistent myth, decades old now, that the signs in municipal parks of foreign-administered Shanghai read: 'Chinese and Dogs Not Admitted'. The factual accuracy of the signs has become irrelevant when the legend thrives, but the neo-imperialism of the Shanghai expatriate community was often stark and unmistakable. When I protested on behalf of my students at the Shanghai Literary Festival, my relationship with the organizers never recovered to our previous collegiality.

The M on the Bund and the Glamour Bar closed in 2021, and with it, the Shanghai International Literary Festival.

Which was a pity, as it brought wonderful writers to Shanghai. In 2009, my debut novel was longlisted for the Man Asian Literary Prize, but the prize went to Chinese writer Su Tong for *The Boat to Redemption* (河岸), translated into English by Howard Goldblatt.

I met Su Tong at the Shanghai International Writers Festival. Su Tong is best known to Western audiences for his novella, *Raise the Red Lantern*, which was adapted into a successful 1991 movie, but I had read *Rice* in my twenties and had been seared by its Zolaesque brutality. I was fangirling, and when Su Tong was exiting the hall after his talk, I stopped him to introduce myself.

His translator explained to him that I wanted to congratulate him as we had both been considered for the Man Asian Literary Prize, and I was a huge fan, and it was an absolute honour, for me, to even be on the same list, and to then to lose to a wonderful writer I had admired for years.

Su Tong looked confused. Then his face broke into a wide grin. He grasped my hand earnestly.

'It is a mistake,' he said in halting English. 'You should have won.'

The interpreter and I both laughed.

'No, no,' he protested earnestly. '*You* should have won.'

He had a fan in me for life.

Su Tong's graciousness was what we received in China from the Chinese; there was a genuine curiosity about India and Indians. At SISU, I was astonished that a large number of my students knew Kalidasa's *Shakuntala* in translation, as it was taught in school. At a diner along Hongmei Lu, a waiter quoted Tagore's poetry to me, then followed it up with Whitman.

We would watch the Bund lights go on at the colonial (old) side at seven in the evening while the clock tower chimed its music, and often, the Chinese tourists would want to take a picture with us. The word Bund is from the same root as the Hindustani word meaning 'embankment', a cognate of English 'bind'. There is a wonderful cosmopolitanism in this area, where the migrating Baghdadi Jews like the Sassoon family settled their businesses in Shanghai from Bombay (now Mumbai) and other ports in east Asia in the nineteenth century.

I found atmospheric teahouses in Shanghai to write in and steeped myself in the Shanghai of the 30s; a bit of sin, crimped hair and starched collars, flowers unfurling in teas and music on scratchy gramophones. I fell in love with Zhujiajao's ancient water village and its smelly tofu.

In all my wanderings, I started to hear the distinctiveness of the Shanghai dialect, which is one of the most representative of the Wu dialects. If a speaker in Shanghai speaks only the Shanghai dialect and tries to speak to someone who knows only Putonghua, they are not able to converse with each other. However, if they are both literate, they can communicate through a shared writing system, that is, simplified Chinese characters. It astonished me initially how literate everyone in China was, used as I was to lower levels of literacy in Indian towns and cities. *Smoke and Mirrors: An Experience of China* by Pallavi Aiyar, offers one of the best analyses for why it is better to be poor in China than India, as China offers greater social mobility and less of the dehumanizing effects of poverty.

My SISU students grew up in environments where they were permitted only to speak Putonghua in elementary schools. A large proportion of my students were training to be teachers of English, which offered greater social mobility in the globalization of China.

* * *

In the typhoon, the trees blur framed
in pagoda windows. The wind whips
picturesque. Rain sheets down an

elemental violence, sheathing the world
emerald green. On ancient waterways
float carved wooden bridges criss–
crossing a feng-shui pathway to
deflect evil spirits. These have borne
lovers and poets, a ghostly
voice—the high trill of a girl—hangs
in the mist like a song.

We travelled to many places in China, but the most memorable was the trip to Tibet. We flew to Xian, the city at the start of the Silk Road, the world's earliest experiment in globalization, and visited the terracotta warriors. Then next day we went by train from Xian to Lhasa, a journey that took thirty-six hours, four of us in a cabin. At one point we were so high above sea level that oxygen was pumped into the cabins to help us breathe. The tracks, laid on permafrost, were a marvel of engineering.

Tibet's hills are magnificent, with nestled turquoise lakes so deep with minerals that their colours seem to light up the skies. Such waters are sacred; Tibetans immerse their dead and don't eat the fish that feed on ancestors. Buddhism came to the land through the porous mountain passes of the Indian subcontinent, through the reverence of monks like Hsüan-tsang who walked from China to India to find the source of knowledge.

The Chinese soldiers at the Potola Palace marched with loud boots down the surrounding avenues lined with prostrating believers. The countrymen were prostrating and sliding on a pilgrimage that took them up to nine months to complete. In the cold crisp air of January, I saw the countryfolk gathered in iridescent silver belts over gathered skirts, their matted hair crowning proud foreheads.

The roads to their Mecca are now lined with signs in Chinese letters; rigid straight lines with flailing arms. The Tibetan script gently flows around prayer bells and circles mandalas, the serifs merging one letter to the next.

We went in the low season, a time when the tourists keep away from the frosty bite in the air, although this was, truly, the most blessed time in Tibet, with the pilgrims jostling in the streets. We were the only tourist family climbing the Potola Palace, our pace unhurried, but our breathing so belaboured that we were clearly set apart from the men and women who navigated the 2,564 steps of the Patola Palace with the gait of mountain goats. One of our teenagers bounded ahead with a camera while the other casually closed his hand around my husband's elbow, discreetly in his aid. My husband found the altitude difficult despite being primed with Hongjingtian and Gaoyuanan to counter altitude sickness at 3,000 metres.

I looked nervously up at the towering roof of the palace, my breathing too difficult to continue a real conversation with the guide. At a break in the steps, the Tibetan women gathered in a huddle—a cheerful, curious group who fingered the cloth of my skirt, their weathered faces and silver belts and headdresses glowing in the sun. One took off her belt, miming an exchange with my bag, and I laughed away the request, grasping her hand to express my gratitude.

Their country was trading in cultural annihilation; tourists like us paid for the burnt manuscripts peddled in the flea markets for a few dollars, the edges smoky and artistically ashen, the words unreadable to the buyers who understand nothing of what is being lost.

Our guide spoke of atrocities in the open air, away from the bugged car, far from restaurants where ears could overhear traitorous conversations. However the changing landscape was

clear in the Han features of the population being brought into
the area by the trains and the signages on the streets.

In Shanghai, when Tibet was mentioned in the English
media at all, it was to point out that Buddhist monasteries were
fiefdoms, and the Dalai Lama was a religious dictator. Taboo
topics I could not discuss in the classroom—ever—included
the Dalai Lama and Tibet, the Falun Gong, Taiwan and
Tiananmen Square.

* * *

Newspaper headlines have too much
death. The guilty in the melamine-milk-scandal
executed. A party official taking bribes
executed. Muslim rebels fighting in Urumqi
executed. There's talk of that drunk driver
being in the gallows soon.

The heart stops too easily here.

Even blood
spilt on white porcelain
starts looking like calligraphy.

I grew to deeply love Shanghai. There was freedom
in being able to come home late from a writers' meeting
downtown, walk on any street alone and unafraid, the children
returning from schools safe from a crazed man with a gun.
There were renegade literary meetings, a very different beast
from the fancy international festival, where we clambered up
rickety ladders to get into huge warehouse spaces within which
edgy poetry and prose was translated into multiple languages.
The lights would go out sometimes, the space felt dangerous

and thrilling. I got to know local Chinese writers, not just the expatriates writing in English. My work was translated into Mandarin.

My students started to write papers on language policy, and the Shanghai dialect, in ways that seemed more honest. In 2012, the Shanghai Academy of Social Sciences released a report which announced that 40 per cent of local Shanghai children are not able to communicate in the Shanghai dialect and Putonghua had become the default language for local adolescents. Large-scale sampling surveys showed that within the family domain, the Shanghai dialect was still being widely used in Shanghai.

In my classroom, the robustness of the Shanghai dialect came as no surprise to students who already knew that multilingualism is a fact of life in most of the world. Speakers do not have to be monolingual for their language to survive.

In addition to papers on the Shanghai dialect, students wrote about the misogynistic language of talent shows, the coded messages of TV presenters in Mongolian borders and how dialect rights intersect with questions on dealing with new internet languages and foreign borrowings. There were robust discussions on preserving and promoting the Shanghai dialect while keeping up with the many demands of a changing local and global linguistic landscape. At times, the classroom reeked of the forbidden.

I left with a strong impression of the distinct and favourable conditions for dialect protection in Shanghai, which included the economic development of dialect areas and the prevalence of diversity in this growing city. Shanghai locals, like the students at SISU, are more willing to speak in the Shanghai dialect than people of other dialects. Putonghua is most likely to be used when talking about business at workplaces and least likely to be used at home.

A backward economy, rather than the mastery of a widely-used language, leads to dialect abandonment, and as Shanghai continues to flourish, the economic robustness is closely related with people's willingness to use their dialect. In China, especially when other factors such as religion are not salient, people from rich places such as Guangdong, Shanghai and Beijing are much more eager to argue for dialect protection.

I left Shanghai with great sadness, knowing that even if I return, it will be for brief stints as a tourist. I will never again be swallowed into a part of that spirit of Shanghai—海纳百，有容乃大—All rivers run into the sea, its greatness contains everything.

A Messiah in Malaysia

Death visits us in different forms. Sometimes it holds your head down in the water and then, inexplicably, lets you go.

Kuantan, Malaysia, 1989. As newlyweds, we were slumming it out on a beach resort. It wasn't the kind with a pool and French cuisine—instead, there were shacks on stilts with grass roofs and a mosquito net to keep the swarming bugs away at night. The front door opened to the whispering susurrations of the South China Sea; the back door looked over an ancient Muslim cemetery with frugal headstones jutting out of fetid ground.

We went swimming with a local guide. Mohan was a large Tamilian, whose lumbering shape belied his ability to swim through the water as if he had fins. The seafood served at the hawker stall by the beach had traces of sand, but it washed down quite well with Tiger beer. We weren't at all bothered when the waiter told us that three teenagers had died on this beach two days ago, sucked into one of the whirlpools, which lurked beneath the placid waters. It was a day of bright sun on blue waters reflecting a clear sky. We wallowed in the warm water to surface briefly for a cool drink or a spicy bite, then kept running back through the powdery sand into a gently heaving sea.

The evening sun had dipped lower in the horizon when the waves came in, the tide slow at first, and then insistently pulling us away from the shore with every exhalation of the sea. By the end of the day, this rocking motion felt soporific, even as it pulled us far from shore. Suddenly, Mohan was a dark speck in the vast ocean as the beach retreated, very far away.

Panicked, we swam towards the shore but the pull of the sea was inexorable. My husband, never a strong swimmer, started to tire. In the salt water, it became easier to pull him up by his hair as his body grew increasingly limp. It is strange how the mind disengages—two months ago, a relative had died in a Delta air crash in Detroit, leaving behind a bride of six months, and I remember watching my husband fight the water and wondering how I would tell his family. Watching my husband struggle to the surface, I thought, *How does any woman tell her in-laws that their son was dead?*

There was no doubt in my mind that I would survive. That I would survive without him, already felt like an unbearable burden.

Then there was a speck of wet blond hair swimming towards us, and a man miraculously appeared by our side. Without asking whether we needed help, he towed us both to safer waters with powerful strokes. When he asked, *Is there anyone else?* I could only point to Mohan, now a bobbing head on the horizon, and our saviour disappeared into the sea. We learnt later, after Mohan was found exhausted but still alive, and people helped us to the local hospital, that our benefactor was a Hawaiian lifeguard vacationing in Kuantan. Although none of the people on the beach could hear our cries for help, he had read our body language from the distance of the beach and known of our distress.

We scoured the hotels in the area but we had a description created out of our terrified minds, not even a name, and we never found him.

It has been twenty-one years since that day, yet I still marvel at how close the margins are between death and life. Each anniversary is sweeter because of our memory of that day in Kuantan; it is a memory which surfaces easily when a child dashes across a busy street or an old man starts to choke on a morsel in his throat. Never take love for granted.

But most of all, the incident in Kuantan taught me the value of this Malay pantun:

> *Hutang emas boleh di bayar, hutang budi di bawa mati.*

> *Debts of gold can easily be repaid/but debts of gratitude are carried to the grave.*

Some debts are indeed carried to the grave.

Dance of the Flyers

It started with the flute.

I had landed in Guadalajara, then taken a thirty-five-minute taxi ride through the verdant green countryside, and now, ensconced in a room a few steps away from Lake Chapala, in a Mecca for artists and writers, within a historic edifice where D.H. Lawrence had composed his awful novel in the 1920s, *The Plumed Serpent*, I could hear, from my balcony, a haunting, melodious tune floating through the palm trees.

In the land of Mariachis, with vihuela and guitarrón and strident violins and trumpets, this muted high treble whispered across the breeze like a finger furled, an invitation, *follow me.* I had grown up with the stories of the dark-skinned god Krishna and his mesmerizing flute that was the siren song for women, and this melody, another lute, ebbed and rose in the breeze even as the hint of a new moon climbed in the night sky and I tried to fall asleep, exhausted by travel, in a new bed in a new country.

The next morning, it was the flute that I woke up to. This time, I followed the sound past the balcony, down the colourful steps, until, at the edge of Lake Chapala, I saw them dancing the Danza de los Voladores.

The Dance of the Flyers, also called the Flying Pole, is an ancient Mesoamerican ritual still performed in pockets in Mexico. They can be found represented in art as background colour: in a painting[2] from the 1690s, there are dancers in exquisitely detailed finery from a wedding in the foreground and the Voladores in the background, suspended upside-down in the air, swinging towards the ground, the pole rising to the sky. In the 1836 hand-coloured lithograph published by Carl Nebel—titled *Indios de la Cierra de Guauchinango*[3] —there are four figures on a hill, the lone man fixated on the spectacle of the Voladores in the far distance.

My first sight of the group of Flying Dancers was also from a distance. By the time I followed the flute sound to the source, five dancers were already on the top of a thirty-metre metal pole, a height which looked reckless from the ground, without any nets spread to break a fall. The central figure, the one who had climbed the serrated steps up the pole last, was the flautist.

This ritual is believed to have originated with the Nahua, Huastec and Otomi peoples in central Mexico, and then spread throughout most of Mesoamerica. The ritual remains consistent: The men dance around the pole, changing directions a few times, then take turns climbing up the pole. The flautist climbs up last, then continues to play the drum and the flute simultaneously, while the other four men harness themselves to long ropes curled around their waist and legs, and thus secured, launch themselves off the top ledge to slowly spiral to the ground. The fifth remains on top of the pole, and continues to play the flute and the drum until the others, with an elegant backflip that brings them down on the ground and walking around the pole in a circle, brings the ceremony to a close.

---

[2] Originally published in Carl Nebel, *Voyage pittoresque et archéologique dans la partie la plus intéressante du Mexique par C. Nebel, Architecte. 50 Planches Lithographiées avec texte explicatif.*, Paris: Chez M. Moench, imprimé chez Paul Renouard; 1836.

[3] Ibid

The men are resplendent in white shirts and black boots and exquisite beaded embroidery on red cloth that drapes over their shoulders and around their waists. In between the dance, they sit at the side, selling trinkets. A couple of the men continue to embroider on red cloth, their carmine canvases blooming with visions of fauna and birds, including the quetzal, a bird that during mating season grows twin tail feathers to form a technicolour train up to a metre long.

As they spin to the ground, I realize that I am watching with bated breath precisely because there is such danger in what they are doing, a danger there for all dancers. The ropes spin the dancers closer to the ground in dizzying circles, then just as it seems a head will surely smash on the ground, the dancers gracefully backflip and are on their feet again.

Yet in this entire dance, and the group selling the trinkets, there is not a single woman. No girl child jostles the men from the side, no woman sits embroidering birds and flowers. This is only the men, and when it is time again, they hoist themselves up the pole and soar into the skies.

Why, I wonder, are their women not soaring too?

* * *

I had an immensely privileged Indian girlhood. As the only daughter in the family of three brothers, the only daughter of a venerated father who overcame his birth in a village so impoverished it had no schools (in the country that is now Bangladesh) to be a successful diplomat in the world's glittering capitals, I was educated in international schools where it was demonstrated, very early on, that no race or gender was superior to my own, and not to my intellect. The teenage years brought restrictions on my movements (my mother's recurrent threat was to marry me off at eighteen so that I would be wed before any boyfriend had the chance to shoot my slutty body dead), but there was nothing that my parents could do to really curtail my freedom, and my practised deception about my whereabouts took care of the rest. I could take on any man in an argument, and I frequently did, for at home I practised with the many men in my family although my mother could shut me up with a narrow-eyed glare.

When I was fourteen, my father was posted back to headquarters again, and we moved from New Zealand, to New Delhi. There was a brief cultural adjustment, especially as my father insisted on enrolling me in a Bengali school where I would learn to read and write as fluently as I spoke. Instead of a shock, this was a boost to my teenage sense of self. Instead of being the girl who had started to doubt herself as being on a dance team as the token Asian, or missing out on the main part of the school play that went to a blonde girl, or seeing my carrot-top crush pursue a love less dusky, I transitioned into an environment where I was not only considered attractive, but even the bad boys found me beautiful. At fourteen, that was a heady change, and I wrote about it, wryly looking back as an adult:

Rewound

You were not like the boys who would sneak into class
and leave notes on my desk (smeared chutney and ink),
you were not into bold nor too shy deference,
no wild words, like heartbeats, marched wanton in lines.

I could well comprehend as the foreign-returned
how I reigned with large breasts bred on clean
wholesome air
Delhi's smog had not marked me, nor Indian sun,
(though my glowing complexion would brown in
six months).

As a veteran of crushes, I already knew
of the heartbreak—and titillation—of the dark side.

I could not bewitch you, not even a sly glance,
when in passing I'd slow in pretend nonchalance—
again pass that canteen, stop and go, one more time—
you were fearless with food, dangerous in your fame,
never asked me for notes never whispered at all:
Did you finish that test? Sometime, I . . . can I call?

When we finally held clammy hands in the dark
of the cinema hall still too bright for our needs,
between closed-mouthed kisses your hand wandered, then
stopped, abashed. When I had to return to my home
I could die but you said you would love only me
forever. It took two months to find someone new.

I would hear after years you had been in a jail
(drunk driving? accident? it was too long ago)
I would hear that you were still too different . . . alone . . .
and I'd feel the dark hall, a still wandering hand,
new magic, and the sizzle of endless possibility.

In that first summer of our return, when the Delhi heat
stretched into two unbearably hot months, we went to Kolkata,
to spend the holidays in a village called Kalyangarh in Habra
district, far from the cosmopolitanism of Kolkata, and into a
Bengali heartland. In this village home lived my father's family,
his elder brother, my Jethu (with his wife with two sons and two
daughters, a third daughter was already married by then), and
another brother, my Sonakaku, who was such a curmudgeon
that he was single.

Kalyangarh was the village home where the outhouse was
a distance away from the main house so that late-night nature

calls were out of the question. Electricity had barely reached the area, and we spent nights lit by the flickering flame of a hurricane lamp which we carried from room to room. Roads were not tarred, but stretched, like a snaky speed bump of scaly red bricks, longitudinally into the distance. Bicycles and carts and hand-drawn rickshaws took us where we wanted to go.

There was no trash disposal system. Kitchen waste went into the ground, the hair from our combs was flung into the pineapple patch growing outside the bedroom window where it would sink to the earth or be carried by the breeze. When I needed to dispose of sanitary napkins, I'd wrap them in paper and fling them outside the window, where they would lie for days, unwrapped and disgusting, until my mother scolded me into burying them deep into the earth.

And suddenly in what felt like a time-warp in many ways, two things happened simultaneously: I became hyperconscious of being an upper-caste Brahmin in an environment which kept the castes resolutely separate, a place where there were very strict rules on the mingling of the sexes and religions; and I was subject to random comments about how rules did not apply to us, because we had already crossed the forbidden seas, and my father was who he was ... we were all *foreign*.

People remarked on the fact that I walked like Indira Gandhi. That had less to do with how I actually walked like the reigning premier of India at that time, and more with how I faced anyone speaking to me, and my strides were not shortened. It was my confidence that was remarkable here in Habra in a way it wasn't at all in metropolitan Delhi. We were about to have a woman Prime Minister in India for the second time, but here women knew their place, and it wasn't one of power.

I met a man on the bus.

When my cousin, Chordi, older than me by a decade, whispered at night that she had met a man on the bus she took to her college every day, I nuzzled closer, delighted at these

womanly secrets being unfurled into my virgin ears. Fed on a
steady diet of Mills and Boons and now reading Jackie Collins
and Harold Robbins, I asked her what he looked like, how they
met, how often they met.

What I was really curious about was how they touched. She
looked astonished.

I only see him on the bus.

There was a lot of *that look* that girls brought up in Indian
cinema know well, that lingering yearning that needs no words,
or even touch, often exchanged across rooms, the length of long
rooftops on summer evenings, and yes, across a crowded bus.

They had talked, yes, as she took the bus daily to go to
college, where she was studying for a bachelor's degree in
biology. She wanted to teach, perhaps for a few years, until it
was time for marriage.

I wanted to meet him. She looked at me as if I was a fool.

Nothing will come out of this. He is of another caste.

Then she grew frightened, and I saw the terror in her eyes.

*Promise me, promise me you will not repeat this conversation to
anyone, you will not tell anyone about him!*

I nodded slowly.

*If you tell anyone, they will get me married off immediately and
I won't be able to go to college any more! Promise!*

I promised. Two years earlier, I had seen another cousin
cuddling with her Kashmiri boyfriend in a darkened movie
hall; they were being so discreet that the only reason I knew
something was going on was because the man's hand brushed
my hair inadvertently as he reached for my cousin, then both
sprang away from each other staring resolutely at the screen and
saying nothing.

That cousin had an arranged marriage the next year, to a
Bengali man of the same caste. This is how it was done. When a
man marries out of his caste, his choice is tolerated, for his wife

and children take on his lineage. A girl wanting to marry out only brought shame to the family and must be stopped.

* * *

In Chapala, I watch the Danza de los Voladores performed multiple times during the day by the men. While it is performed, a member of the team goes around holding the distinctive headgear and collects the change that tourists see fit to spare.

What looks like a commercial enterprise now, has deeply religious roots. According to myth, this is a ritual to please the rain god, to make the earth fertile again after a severe drought. The dance did not originate with the Totonac people, but today it is strongly associated with them, especially those in and around Papantla in the Mexican state of Veracruz.

I want to talk to the men. Maypole dances are ceremonial folk dances performed in Scandinavian countries, England and Spain and even in my native state of West Bengal. In these very disparate communities, there is the commonality of people dancing around a tall pole garlanded with flowers, often hung with ribbons that are woven into complex patterns by the dancers, sometimes termed as Ribbons of Love. Such dances are survivals of ancient dances around a living tree as part of spring rites to ensure fertility, and originally the maypole was a living tree of the correct height—usually birch or pine in Western countries. In modern pictures of Maypole dances, women are represented, and even children can be seen dancing joyously around a colourfully-festooned centre.

But if this was originally a fertility ritual, even a ritual to welcome the rain to fertilize the earth, why wasn't I seeing women at the Lake Chapala performances?

I have so many questions, but I don't want to come across as a clueless tourist engaged in cultural voyeurism, dishonouring ancient traditions. But I have questions about the commercial practice versus religious roots of this ritual; How far the men travel and how many in their troupe; Whether women are (ever) included; Concerns about safety: Government and community support; Whether the younger generation is moving on to different ways to earn a living; What was their status in their communities (were they representatives of Gods, or mere acrobatic performers?); Whether the dancers have to adhere to any norms before this religious performance . . .

I have so many questions.

I find an interpreter in Michael Pribich, an American artist whose contemporary sculpture—his website tells me—is informed by labour, race, colonialism, immigration issues. Michael has been learning Spanish for years and speaks with confidence. He is, like me, on an artistic residency in Chapala.

Michael introduces me to the dancers as a writer interested in folk traditions like the Voladores. But when we start talking, the men are wary. Michael is not a native speaker of the language and the dancer turns repeatedly to me, telling me yes, they have come from the Veracruz region. I look like someone who would understand Spanish, but I comprehend about 20 per cent of what is said. Desperately searching for cognates through this fog of sound, I answer none of the dancer's questions. Finally, the dancer directs us to speak to someone else in the troupe, another man who keeps his mobile phone to his ear and walks away, and it is made clear that they would rather not talk to us.

* * *

Chordi's biggest fault was that she was dark of complexion, and therefore not conventionally beautiful for the arranged marriage market. Bengalis as a community prize what is termed a 'wheatish complexion', the colour attributed to the domesticated goddesses of Bengal who bless homes and progeny, the Durgas and the Lakshmis.

Chordi's skin tone was of a dark, fearsome Kali. But she struck no terror in anyone who looked upon her.

My father's eldest brother, Chordi's father, had not worked after the Partition of India had left him landless and skill-less, so there was little dowry. An unemployed man in the house for a lifetime brought the entire family together to raise his children; but the daughters of the house must be handed over to another family as soon as they reached marriageable age. That process started as soon as the Indian law allowed it, which was, at that time, when the girls turned eighteen.

When I was sixteen, I saw how an arranged marriage dehumanizes a girl, how her skin, her teeth, her height, her family are openly discussed by complete strangers, decisively and publicly. How a rejection makes the girl's own family turn against her in despair. Prospective grooms came to view Chordi in the homes of relatives in Kolkata; the net was spread wide, but with every male refusal—Chordi was never allowed an opinion—her faults grew monstrous.

The misogyny is the shrillest from the women.

These Mukherjee girls are just unmarriageable, declared an aunt who'd married into our family. *No looks, no talent. No sweetness even. We just have to pay a king's ransom to have someone take them off our hands.*

Chordi had tears in her eyes.

Well, if someone married you, I'm sure finding a groom for Chordi will become easier. I retorted with teenage insolence. There was a heavy silence in the room.

Good thing they at least have a mouth, otherwise the foxes would cart them away as jungli waste. The aunt hissed.

This! This is what happens when you are brought up abroad in heathen countries, you have no culture, no manners, no idea how to speak to elders, to anyone. And with that, the uncle married to the mean aunt circumscribed the deficiencies of my father's parenting, and I was silenced.

Bujhlish, girls are liabilities, and the faster you marry them off, the lesser your loss. Chordi's elder brother told me this the next day, his introductory word making it clear that he was delivering a universal truth. He had so normalized his misogyny that nothing he said riled me any more. He was a bank manager, well-acquainted with the spreadsheets of debit and credit columns. In that year when Chordi whispered about her man-in-the-bus, I had witnessed this brother coming home for a home-made lunch, served by his sisters who had just returned from college, and flinging the brass plate in a vicious spin because the salt was inadequate.

I had fled the scene, the noise of the bell-metal ringing in my ears.

I told myself that there was no way my gentle father would behave like that with any of the women in his family, and my brothers would not only never do something so uncivilized, but they knew my mother and I were likely to break the plate on their heads if they tried. But at the moment it happened in Kalyangargh, I could only think, *there, but for the Grace of God, go I* and I was grateful. Grateful that my father had escaped Kalyangargh to start earning his own living as a homeopathic doctor's assistant at the age of fourteen, and put himself through school, or else I would have been Chordi.

(That this plate-thrower would, decades later, have a single son who would marry a foreigner and live in Europe with a daughter, far away from any such performances of toxic masculinity, makes me think that life stops the patriarchy from perpetuating itself. Even when we, ourselves, are such terrible cowards.

What a long wait for justice that is.)

Finally, a groom who was sufficiently unsuitable was found for Chordi, a man willing to accept a dark girl with insufficient dowry. She married into a large joint family that never stopped reminding her of her own inadequacies and when she failed to conceive after the marriage, it became inevitable that she would become the unpaid nurse for an ailing mother-in-law and the nanny to the many nieces and nephews born in her marital home. But she would never be enough.

I never asked Chordi again about her man-in-the-bus. The one time I tried, the sheer panic in her eyes shut me up. She became a cousin without any secrets, even her skin growing translucent. The diseases started taking over her body, she started bleeding from the inside. In a family that enjoyed general good health, she was the one that they *tsked* over, remarking how good her husband was to keep taking her for medical treatments, when she couldn't give him any happiness, not even a single child.

Did I become a writer because of the Chordis in my life? People that I watched helplessly because I was too young, too voiceless at the time? In my fiction, Chordis elopes with the-man-in-the-bus, teaches biology in a college, and becomes someone no one pities.

To be completely fair in my telling of Chordi's story, I also have to acknowledge that during this time I also knew of women who flouted tradition, married outside caste and community, and rebelled against constraints. It takes a certain intrepidity to accept excommunication from the community and exile from family as the price for personal happiness, but the price is not an early death.

What of the wounds we collectively carry, and interact as if we don't?

Maybe I just want this story to be about courage. About rage. And I am making it about voicelessness because I can give Chordi a voice if I claim she had none.

* * *

I turn to research about the Voladores, especially about the exclusion of women.

The Danza de los Voladores is often associated with the Totonacs of the Papantla area in Veracruz. According to the Totonac myth, the Gods told the men, 'Dance, and we shall observe' and this ritual still retains an intensely religious heart. The dress is traditional. I observed the embroidered red pants with a white shirt, gloriously embroidered cloth across the chest—symbolizing blood—and a colourful cap. The hat has flowers for fertility, mirrors representing the sun and multicoloured ribbons representing the rainbow. The Voladores, in between performances, still sit deftly embroidering parts of these costumes by hand.

Traditionally, the ritual started with the selection, cutting and erecting of the tree to be used. Called the *tsakáe kiki*, it involved finding a suitable tree and asking the permission and pardon of the mountain god Quihuicolo for taking it (the Malay archipelago records similar rituals for asking permission and pardon before desecrating the earth in anyway, like breaking the ground in preparation to planting). A hole is dug and offerings of flowers, copal, alcohol, candles and live chickens or a live turkey are placed in the hole before the tree trunk is planted, stripped of all the branches. The offerings are symbols of the fertility of the earth, and the pole becomes a representation of the world tree, connecting the earth and sky, this world and the others.

Nowadays, just as I observed in Chapala, the pole is permanently placed, and made of steel. It still carries the heft of a religious totem, for not once in my time in Chapala did I see anyone, not even a runaway child, trying to climb this pole for just the fun of it. Due to the deforestation of much of the mountain areas of Veracruz, most Voladores perform on these permanent metal poles.

The ritual is no longer performed for religious purposes only. In smaller communities, the ritual is still enacted only on the feast day of the community's patron saint or other religious events, but in larger cities especially with large tourist attractions, this ritual is performed for tourist money. The first organization for Voladores was formed in the 1970s which was when this ritual was facing more commercialization—there are approximately 600 professional Voladores in Mexico now—and groups of Voladores are trying to balance respect for the ritual while still performing for spectators.

However, the most controversial issue for the Voladores has been the induction of women to perform the ceremony. Traditionally barred from participation in this ritual, some women have started to become Voladores, and all are in the Puebla state.

Jesús Arroyo Cerón, aged seventy, died when he fell from a pole during the Cumbre Tajín 2006 cultural festival. In an article available online at *jornada.com*, Andres Morales writes that one of the vines apparently burned his hands, and Jesús let go about ten metres before he hit the ground. Jesús Arroyo Cerón was among the first to train women to become Voladores; he trained his daughter Isabel in 1972, then he trained his other three daughters. When he fell from a pole and died, family members believed he fell 'at the side of the Gods', and a wooden cross and flowers at the Plaza del Volador in Parke Takilhsukut memorialize his passing.

Others, including the elders of the Totonacs, believed the death of Cerón to be divine retribution. They prohibited the performance of the ritual by any other women participants. Despite this injunction, about twenty female Voladores are known to persist. In a few communities, such as Cuetzalan and Pahuatlán in Puebla and Zozocolco de Hidalgo in Veracruz, women continue to train as Voladores, but only after completing a series of rituals designed to ask the forgiveness of the Gods and the Catholic saints.

The women must be virgins without a boyfriend if unmarried. Or, if married, she must abstain from sexual relations before the ritual. A female Volador caught breaking the rules of sexual abstention is taken to an altar which is surrounded by incense burners and candles. There, in front of the image of the Archangel Michael or Saint James, a number of slaps to the face are administered, the severity depending on the transgression and the decision of those in charge. This ritual is carried out to cure an essential 'fever' in women, and any woman who does not obey these rules is thought to invite certain catastrophe.

Variation in dance styles is allowed; the number of performers, whether or not there is a pole ceremony, and sometimes there is no dance before climbing the pole and the ceremony begins at the top. Some dancers fast for one or more days before the ceremony, as well as abstain from sexual relations.

But in Papantla, the community most closely associated with the ritual, where the Council of Totonac Elders has formally prohibited the inclusion of women, even for the dance called *La Maringuilla*, the female protagonist is portrayed by a man.

The Danza de los Voladores ceremony was named an Intangible Cultural Heritage by UNESCO in 2009. A school for Volador children was established and the students learn about the cultural history of the ritual starting from a pre-Hispanic period. Sponsored by the Veracruz state government, the school welcomes children between six and eight years of age, mostly from the neighbouring communities of Voladores. The school requires students to meet language requirements.

But girls are not permitted.

I meet the dancers by Lake Chapala, and pick through the wooden representations of the dance for sale by the Voladores.

I leave the blues and greens and red and choose a brown pole with five Voladores, most clearly representative of a real tree pole. A young man, the child of one of the performers, helps me pick one out.

He has Down's Syndrome. He does not perform, but he points excitedly to the Voladores with the flute at the top of the pole in the souvenir I hold in my hand.

That's me, he says in Spanish so expressive that I have no trouble understanding. He mimics holding a flute and points to his own chest and the figure on top of my memento again and again.

The other performers mill around, smiling indulgently. As a male child, he is allowed to dream.

* * *

I already said my Chordi had dusky skin, the worst thing a girl can be in the arranged marriage market.

My Chordi was dark, yes, but also beautiful in a way beyond the conventional beauty standards of Bollywood. She was always slim, but in her fifth decade of life as her ill-health persisted, she became model-thin. Her body, unstretched by childbearing, remained taut. Her skin glistened.

The leading goldsmiths of Kolkata, a veritable empire whose huge hoardings towered over every highway and bypass, recruited Chordi as a model. Her images didn't tower over the stalled cars in Kolkata's traffic jams, but were printed in fliers, and distributed to local showrooms. Gold glittered against Chordi's dark skin, for even the mannequins in this goldsmith's fancy Gariahat and Ballygunge showrooms were a deep shade of chocolate.

For a while, Chordi was very happy. I tried, from the US, to find pictures of her online, glittering in the artisanal designs the showrooms were famous for, but I found nothing. She sent the fliers to my mother, showed her the pictures pasted into a scrapbook.

Then, suddenly, Chordi passed away. Too soon, in her early sixties. She was the youngest of five siblings in her family, but the first one to die.

Within two years of her passing, her husband, still youthful, started looking for a new mate. He asked his entire network, including our family—his former in-laws—to help him find a suitable bride.

It would have been inconceivable that if Chordi had been widowed, she would have gone to her husband's family to entreat them to find her a new mate. I was incensed, that even in death, she would be so replaceable; that even her own family, her brothers, all of us, would be complicit in finding her substitute.

But wasn't that what the entire arranged marriage system is premised on? If not one bride, then any other would do equally well? It is only the man's lineage, his seed to be sown in a fertile field, that is of any value. More so for upper-caste Brahmin families like mine, where the women are equally complicit in upholding the patriarchy in the name of tradition.

* * *

In Chapala, when I return to the Voladores the next day, it is with the Columbian artist, Esperanza Cortes. She is married to Michael. Esperanza is charming, and speaks fluently to the Voladores, making it clear that she is Columbian, with a mixed heritage though she looks Caucasian. She laughs and says that she sometimes has to search for words in Spanish, signalling to the dancers that, just like them, she speaks another mother tongue.

The men respond enthusiastically. They wax poetic about family lineages being strong in this ritual, about abuelos and ninos continuing the tradition equally, stress that it is a part of their shared heritage, so of course it'll continue. They point to sons and nephews in the group. It is a family enterprise.

When Esperanza broaches the topic of women, they give terse replies. There was an accident. Girls are forbidden. The mood shifts.

We buy some souvenirs as we make small talk, then stand and watch as the dancers—the 'bird men'—start circumambulating the pole in order to please the Gods. The flute is the voice of birds, the dancers clambering up a World Tree. The flautist first bows to the East, the origin of the world, the place of the sun. I read that each person turns thirteen times around the pole, for thirteen circles multiplied by the four dancers is a total of fifty-two circles, signifying the Mayan calendar, where fifty-two years make a solar cycle. Fifty-two weeks is a year, which results in the birth of a new sun so that life may go on.

I lose track of trying to count, and just enjoy the spectacle of the men spinning in the mild sunshine by the blue waters.

A sixteenth-century Franciscan friar, Juan de Torquemada, documented the Indian practice of erecting a 'flying mast' at major festivals. One can assume that strident missionary attempts to halt this practice stemmed from concerns about the worship of heathen Gods as well as the spectacle of public deaths, for the published English translation of *Del palo volador de que usaban estos indios en sus fiestas principals* describes the ritual in much detail.[4]

---

[4] The translation can be found in Woodruff, John M. 'Flying Indians [Regarding the flying mast that the Indians used in their major festivals].' *Iconic Mexico: An Encyclopedia from Acapulco to Zócalo*. Ed. Eric Zolov. Vol. 2. Santa Barbara, USA: ABC-CLIO, 2015. 664–666.

> Among other celebratory practices that these western Indians had was an acrobatic custom—flying through the air on tethers that hung from a tall, sturdy wooden mast with which those in attendance eased their spirits and deepened the solemnity of their gatherings—and I will [now] describe its substance in words for the amusement of the reader . . .

The Indians that flew were not altogether special, but rather they simply were very well trained for the job . . . and at a Festival of Saint James that was celebrated in Tlatelulco this past year of 1611 (the second time it was done since I left that church), an Indian fell from the top and died in the fall; and at this point in time others have died and other disasters and tragedies have occurred; yet even this is not sufficient deterrent, any more than it is to deter bullfighting to see that each time that they are performed there are injuries and deaths of men in bull rinks, because as the saying goes, even though one ship be lost at sea, they allow the others to sail.

Don Jesús Arroyo was not the first man to fall to his death while dancing at this ritual, and certainly not the last. Yet his death continues to be the reason to bar women's participation from this culturally and religiously symbolic dance. In another article at *jornado.com*, Morales describes how the Totonac women continue to fight to be a part of the ritual, despite being excluded from the dance rituals of the community, as they were 'sinful beings' who would surely invite the wrath of the Gods for their audacity.

Don Jesús Arroyo's daughter, trained by her father, first began dancing in 1972, after convincing her father to teach her to fly. Morales quotes Isabel as saying, 'There was no permission for women to fly and my father, after begging him a lot, agreed to teach me, almost secretly. We rehearsed in a tree.'

Isabel's three sisters followed her example. But even now, half a century after Jesús first taught his daughters, female participation in the Voladores is limited; only in Zozocolco de Hidalgo and in Cuetzalan, are there Totonac women flying.

Viviana Guerrero García was taught by Doña Isabel Arroyo. She describes how she has always wanted to fly, since she was a little girl, and trained hard to keep her balance, tie her limbs to the rope and jump into the void.

'Open your arms and fly; in the flight you contact God, you turn for him. The dance of women is as good as that of men, it is worth the same before the Gods. We also know how to fly like birds.'

* * *

My last full day in Chapala was on 15 August 2022, a day that also marked seventy-five years of Indian Independence from British rule, an unshackling of the country still celebrated with imperial pomp and splendour.

Indian Prime Minister Narendra Modi addressed the nation with a plea: 'I have one request to every Indian: Can we change the mentality towards our women in everyday life? It is important that in our speech and conduct, we do nothing that lowers the dignity of women.'

It felt like a heartfelt plea in a country where female foeticide is rampant, despite the laws and penalties against it. A girl-child, especially in an arranged marriage, is still a liability in terms of the dowry expected. There are the dowry deaths, the terminology native to India and her daughters, referring to the murder or suicide of a married woman caused by a dispute over her dowry. In the majority of these suicides, women take their lives by hanging, poisoning or self-immolation. When a dowry death involves setting the woman on fire—by her husband or in-laws—it is termed bride burning.

Dowry is illegal in India, as it already was in 1961, more than two decades before I watched the trials Chordi went through to find a suitable Brahmin groom, not only of the right caste, but also the matching subcaste.

On the day that Prime Minister Modi asked Indians to start treating women with dignity, on the same day on 15 August, eleven Brahmin convicts who were serving life sentences for rape and murder in the case involving a Muslim woman, walked out of prison in Gujarat to a heroes' welcome. These eleven convicts had been convicted by a Special Central Bureau of Investigation (CBI) court in 2008 for the gang rape of a Muslim woman, Bilkis Bano, and the murder of seven of her family members during the 2002 Gujarat riots and were given life sentences, but now, they walk free.

A Bharatiya Janata Party minister, who was on the committee that recommended the 'remission' defended the convicts with the argument that they were Brahmin men and therefore had good moral character. A clear dog whistle in a country growing increasingly intolerant of minorities and the rights of women.

Caste—especially when the perpetrator is Brahmin—is being normalized as evidence of being above the law. Especially when the crime is against a woman.

For me, it felt like an enormous bell metal plate being flung on my heart when I watched the video of the rapists being released. The footage of the men as heroes went viral, and anyone could watch the saffron scarves draped ceremoniously around convicted necks, the adulation of those respectfully touching their feet, the rapists being garlanded like Gods.

The Indian Supreme Court, as expected, issued notices on a clutch of petitions challenging the remission of the convicts, but it is also important to remember that Narendra Modi was once barred from the US in 2005 for failing to stop anti-Muslim riots. He was, for nearly a decade, prohibited from setting foot on American soil, and that 2005 decision by the US government was based on Modi's failure to stop a series of deadly riots by Hindus against minority Muslims in the Indian state of Gujarat, where he was chief minister at that time. The US State Department invoked a little-used US law passed in 1998 that made foreign officials responsible for 'severe violations of religious freedom' ineligible for visas.

Modi is now the Prime Minister of India, leading a nation where the growing Hindutva movement is all about religious fanaticism, and propping up the power of upper-caste Hindus. Despite his public posturing, the freeing of the eleven convicts on the same day of his speech, as the government continues to jail activists and dissenters for long stretches, shows an India that is disinclined to allow women justice or equality in the eyes of the law, making India even more unsafe for women, and more so for Muslim women. This will only serve the patriarchy to keep more women confined to the home; female workforce participation in India is among the lowest in the world and continues to fall. Before the pandemic, the female participation rate was at 42 per cent, now it has fallen to 39.9 per cent.

Yet Indian women scientists have already proven they can send a mission to Mars, soaring beyond any of the confines of Earth.

I can no longer be of any use to my Chordi, even though I now have a voice. The banning of women from a religious rite and the raping or killing of women is not the same thing, but women around the world continue to wrestle with being controlled and diminished in multiple ways, by being forced into lives not of their own choosing. I want women to be able to choose their own danger, like men do, in marriage and choice of career. I want my words to be the flute, the siren-call of birds, cheering young women, every one of them, wherever they are in this world, to clamber up the World Tree unfettered, because they can.

Terrorism Finds No Room Here

The first time I attended the Irrawaddy Literary Festival in Mandalay in 2014, I was dazzled. Irrawaddy. Mandalay. Bagan. The words tripped off the tongue poetically, redolent of Rudyard Kipling read on wide tropical verandas in the monsoon. Mandalay is home to the Kuthodaw Pagoda, a Buddhist stupa known for containing the world's largest book; 729 pristine white domes stretch to the horizon as far as the eye can see, each containing a marble slab inscribed on both sides with a page from the Buddhist collection of scriptures, the Tripitaka. A bibliophile's dream, it is like walking in the middle of an ancient open book.

This festival, in its second year in 2014, was blessed by the patronage of Aung San Suu Kyi. It felt like the G8 of literary festivals, run like a diplomatic summit by the staff of the British Embassy and various literary organizations around Myanmar.

That Suu Kyi was an alumna of the same elite New Delhi college I attended as an undergrad, was an added thrill in this historical festival that was opening up Myanmar to the international literary world. Burma, as Myanmar was formerly known, features in the Bengali literature written by Sarat Chandra and Rabindranath Tagore and other luminaries, and I grew up in this land of many-splendored things. Burma was the 'Suvarnabhumi', a part of a fabled golden land in ancient Sanskrit texts.

A memory of the Burma teak bed in my grandparent's home, an uncle who made his fortune in this country long before I was born . . . this festival felt like a homecoming.

The festival had teething problems, with bureaucratic hurdles placed in the path of the detractors of a popular political figure—the problems persisted through the years. Yet, the organization always rallied valiantly, and in 2014, despite a last-minute change of venue, Suu Kyi showed up in person to discuss her childhood reading habits, and express a special fondness for poetry.

Huge crowds gathered to watch her speak at the festival. Taxi drivers, without exception, sang her praises. Poets read fiery paeans to her, while bemoaning the encroachment of Chinese money into every aspect of life in Myanmar. Even the red-robed monks hotly debated the finer points of politics and social change. In an audience filled with students who were bussed into the venue from surrounding regions, a writer angrily demanded to know why there was a Ministry of Defence, but no Ministry of Peace in our world. Young nuns in light pink robes nodded, and the trendy young volunteers from the Jefferson Centre conducted simultaneous translations for foreign delegates in fluent English, breaking into a giggle when the exchange became too heated to translate.

It was all incredibly thrilling. A Brave New World of Free Speech made possible in one of the most censored countries in Southeast Asia.

* * *

By the time I returned in 2019, Suu Kyi had not lived up to the ideals she represented in 2014—at least not for the international community that found her response to the

Rohingya crisis unforgivable. But the festival had grown, with multiple parallel sessions running concurrently with books in translation from all over the world. Suu Kyi's welcome message was broadcast on giant screens, but she was physically absent in the packed standing-room-only hall.

'To be in a room like this, filled with the people of Myanmar chatting easily to foreign writers who had come from around the world, felt simply unbelievable,' said author Aung Myint in 2014, a member of the organizing committee.

In 2019, the number of panels grew, as did the diplomatic presence. During the launch of a book on regional textiles, the Singaporean ambassador, Vanessa Chan, spoke with great erudition on the history of indigenous weaving techniques in Myanmar, before Mai Ni Ni Aung, a local textile scholar, took the stage to describe, with emotional impact, how dangerous it was becoming to source textiles, especially in the contentious Rakhine state. The Indian Ambassador, Saurabh Kumar, flew from Yangon to hear me speak on teaching creative writing in Asia.

There were many more panels featuring women in 2019. I made lots of friends with writers who were also schoolteachers, lawyers, homemakers and hairdressers. In a panel titled 'Literary Lovers of Myanmar', women began the discussion with an ancient writer who had to give up literature after a royal decree. The panel then highlighted modern examples of women writing under pseudonyms to be read by men, and only men having authority over Buddhist literature. Women were asked questions about whether they needed an evolution or a revolution. Patriarchy was in the air, but so was the indomitable spirit of Suu Kyi.

Now, in Chicago, I watch with horror as poets and thinkers are martyred in Myanmar's protests. I scroll through Facebook posts of writers in Myanmar: pictures of protest sites, protestors sharing lunchboxes, intimations of another internet blackout, pictures of Suu Kyi, pictures of the Buddha and images of broken flowers still in bloom.

I mentored Southeast Asian writers for over two decades now and I know the dangers of self-censorship as well as its naïve twin, the foreign saviour. As a result, I do not comment online. Just when the windows to freedom in Myanmar seemed to be opening, they are being shut in a region with so many stories still untold. In Southeast Asia, even the more mature democracy in Malaysia is grappling with the problem of whether to allow non-Muslims to even use the word Allah.

In 2019, on my final panel on Indian literature and Myanmar, I was with Zaw Thun, a poet and professor at the Mandalay University of Foreign Languages. We exchanged books as goodbye gifts, and I brought home his book of poems, a book filled with heart and hope for Myanmar. In *At the Roadside Magic Show*, he writes:

> *Now Myanmar is like the man inside the box,*
> *being poked by sharp, inhuman spikes after spikes,*
> *tangible and intangible,*
> *from within and outside.*
>
> *Yet, as after the show,*
> *appeared the man from inside the bamboo box*
> *with not a scratch on his body,*
> *So does Myanmar survive safe and sound . . .*
> *terrorism finds no room here.*

For the sake of the many writers I grew to admire in Myanmar, I hope the country emerges unscathed to find a voice—and freedom—again.

Singing about Coronavirus

'Didi'—the driver addresses me as Elder Sister—'if you had come even two weeks ago, you would have seen our fields all golden with wheat. Our land is so beautiful.'

I am on my way to Pingla, home to about eighty-five families of Patachitra painters or Patuas, artisans practising an ancient art form by painting stories in a series of frames on long scrolls of cloth. As they unfurl the scrolls, they sing the stories.

The village is 130 kilometres from Kolkata by road, and I am with Susama Chitrakar—the last name Chitrakar is a family surname that indicates one who makes art—a Patachitra artist who now specializes in painting on social issues. If there is flooding in the Bay of Bengal, or a need to spread awareness about HIV/AIDS, Susama works with an NGO to get the message to the most impoverished and illiterate parts of rural West Bengal. Artists such as Susama don't have showrooms or websites and are struggling through the pandemic, yet they continue to create astonishing work; her talent has been recognized by the Indian government and her work is displayed in exhibitions as far away as China and Norway.

She is part of this unique tribe of folk artists who paint pictures, makeup lyrics to songs to accompany the images, then perform sometimes in front of crowds, sometimes singing to a single person. They are equally at ease narrating mythological stories from Indian epics like the *Ramayana* or singing stories from community lore. In these times, when social messages on the pandemic are a priority, they have quickly adapted, painting stories of hospitals and vaccination needles in a series of frames on long scrolls, like large-print comic books without the text.

Susama is taking me to show me her village and the process of her art. I am interested in seeing how the vivid colours are made, especially as the paint she uses is foraged from the land she lives on.

I met Susama at the Crafts Museum in Delhi in November 2020, two years ago, where she was trying to sell her art at a time when pictures seemed frivolous as sirens screeched through the world's cities, including outside on the roads of Delhi, ferrying the sick and the dying. Susama sat surrounded by a wallpaper of scrolls in a stall made to replicate a mud hut, and in that small space, colours bloomed into the mythology of Hindu Gods, Buddhist animal tales, and Bengali fish marriage motifs.

She turned a scroll around to show me the patterned cotton of a recycled sari on the other side. Then she burst into song:

Ei ki bhoyonkoro holo re coronavirus, ei ki bhoyonkoro!
Coronavirus namey shunini kokhono, ei ki bhoyonkoro!

How frightening is this coronavirus, so frightening!
Never heard of coronavirus before, yet so frightening!

As Susama sang, she rolled the scroll downward, covering the part that looked like a demon—a Rakshash—with gaping mouth swallowing tiny humans. She then pointed to a picture of a TV set, with masked doctors milling around:

TV te joto dekhi toto praney lagey bhoi, ei ki bhoyonkoro!
Boro daktarbabu kabu hoye jai, ei ki bhoyonkoro!

The more I watch TV, the more terrifying it is, so
frightening!
The skilled doctors are felled by this, so frightening!

When she sang about the need to wash hands frequently
with soap, the picture she pointed to was not a tap but a
hand pump. The rural villages of West Bengal are one of the
poorest areas in South Asia, and there is a shortage of clean
and safe drinking water, with people reliant on nearby ponds
for drinking, cooking, bathing, washing, and other day-to-day
activities. During the monsoons, water in these small ponds
becomes even more unsafe and causes many illnesses.

Susama's full-throated song about the need for masks and
distancing was astonishing in its modern references, for she was
using the tune and couplets of oral singers, at times replicating
the repetitive couplets of religious bhajans. The genre would be
familiar to Indians, but her message was startlingly topical.

I sat mesmerized by her cinematic presentation and the
ease with which she delivered it so fluently, like a rap artist
needing nothing written to perform, and sometimes even
riffing. We had started to chat in Bengali, as I had seen the
prominently displayed sign explaining that she was an artist
from West Bengal.

After the coronavirus scroll, she unfurled one with
Goddesses and sang a paean to the Goddess Durga, surrounded
by the Goddesses Kali, Lakshmi, and Saraswati, a pantheon
most beloved in Bengal. It was clearly a practised spiel for a
Bengali tourist, but I was still riveted by her coronavirus scroll.
I asked about the paints used, the recurring religious iconography
in her scrolls, the similarity to the Kalighat style of painting
favoured by the British when India was the jewel in the crown.
Susama urged me to visit Pingla to see how these scrolls are

made, handing me her telephone number to keep in touch. 'Come in November next year,' she said. 'We have the Pat Mela, and the whole village becomes an open-air art gallery!'

* * *

Two years would pass before the pandemic would ease enough to allow me to visit her artisanal village, but finally, in May 2022, I am in a car hired from Kolkata, with Susama by my side.

In the morning, I wake up to views of trees pregnant with bright red lychees next to verdant banana leaves curving their graceful stems over the pond. A bright orange duck shack is identifiable in large English and Bengali script as Hash Ghor and Duck House. A yellow swing waits in the garden.

I stay at the only hotel in the area, listed as a Bagan-Bari, literally translated as Garden-Abode. It is basic but set in a picturesque landscape. The motorized Toto—battery-operated rickshaw—waits for me as breakfast is served, a languid, slow preparation, as everything on my plate is harvested from the land around us—including the duck-egg omelette.

My host is curious about why I want to see the Chitrakars. He has retired to this bucolic life after a successful career in Kolkata and slowly sips his milky tea, indifferent to time passing.

'You have to understand,' he begins, 'these artists, even ten years ago, were selling pictures on the street, at traffic junctions, street corners. No one wanted to buy their stuff. Then the government money started to come in. Once they were *begging* people to buy their art, now people come from overseas and they peddle everything to tourists like you.'

I nod. I already know the artisans make a range of products beyond the scrolls, as I bought T-shirts and face masks and items for home décor with Patachitra motifs from Susama in

Delhi. Patachitra received the Geographical Indication tag, and the government of West Bengal's Department of Micro, Small, and Medium Enterprises & Textiles, in association with UNESCO, developed a rural craft hub in Pingla.

'Their fortunes changed so fast,' my host muses. Then he uses a word I haven't heard used in speech: 'These people, you know, are *Mohammedans.*'

And there it was. His surname identified him as a Bengali Hindu, and mine, as in much of India, gave away my caste, religion, and the region of a (patriarchal) lineage. He was suggesting solidarity in a sharply-divided India, where minorities were under the threat of the growing Hindutva movement. Muslims were the most vilified and frequently thought to take more Indian largesse than was their due.

When I first spoke to Susama in Delhi, we did not speak of her religion at all; her art seemed beyond religion, especially as the message was about a pandemic that was killing so many, all around the world. Despite the majority of her iconography being Hindu, her religion seemed irrelevant to me.

Yet so much about what the Patuas like Susama do is inextricably weighed down by religion, and it has been so for a long time. Susama's family is Muslim. Patuas can be Hindus or Muslims, and all practise customs that are both Hindu and Islamic in nature, and these communities are found in neighbouring Bangladesh as well as in many eastern Indian states including West Bengal. Like many heritage artisanal communities, they are often impoverished and rely largely on Hindu patronage, or from selling art as tourist souvenirs. Many are being forced into jobs as daily wage labourers, or factory workers, leaving them no time for their art.

Although the precise origin of this art form is undocumented, Chitrakars and their art form can historically be traced back to the thirteenth century. Some Chitrakars claim an ancestry that stretches to the artists of cave paintings in the region. The skill of Patachitra is the pride of Bengal; on arrival at the Kolkata airport, people see a huge mural in this style, and the heritage hotel I stayed at had a room styled in this art form.

The Patuas have been a part of Bengal as a unique community that speaks to the diversity at the heart of India. Although their traditional occupation is the painting of Hindu idols, many of them are Muslims and widely known as Chitrakar, which literally means a scroll-painter. Emblematic of the cross-pollination of centuries, Patuas are mentioned in Hindu, Buddhist, and Islamic historical texts, their faith as porous as the art they created.

Often a Patua has two names, one Hindu and one Muslim. When I finally reach Susama's home and she introduces her children to me, her three daughters have Bengali names, unmarked by religion. Only her son introduces himself with a clearly Muslim name.

* * *

The walls pop with colour as Susama bustles about her home, bringing me teapots with fish motifs, small wooden decorated trays, stationery items, and even a hand-painted wedding sari. I am given a mora to sit on, a traditional stool handwoven from bamboo reeds. Susama lives in this home with her four children, her husband, and both her parents.

Her father tells me about generations of his ancestors being scroll painters or Patuas, how they travelled like wandering minstrels selling their scrolls and singing stories in return for a cup of rice, some lentils, maybe a bit of a vegetable, or, on good days, a coin or two. He tells me about the popular religious stories such as the medieval mangal poems and how his work has promoted literacy in surrounding villages.

Father: There are three kinds of light in this world. The light of the sun and the moon, we see that every day, but there is a light within us that is also necessary to illuminate the world.

Me: Light within us?

Father: You know who Kalidas was?

Me: My father was named Kalidas, after the most famous ancient Indian poet and playwright . . . yes, I know.

Father (*pointing to his picture*): This is Kalidas, this is Saraswati. Kalidas was an illiterate thug, but then he learned how to read and write and went on to write marvellous literature like . . .

Me: Shakuntala!

Father: Yes! The next picture is of illiterate village folk, picking up notebooks. Then the final picture is of them learning to write. I use this in villages; I sing about Kalidas, to promote literacy, to show anyone can learn.

Me: Wonderful!

Father: I do it to spread the light. Within all of us. Wherever you can, spread the light.

Her father's scroll has three parts, and the lines are sparse, the characters alike in face and form. Susama's work is much more detailed, clearly more sophisticated in the use of colour and the complexity of recurring motifs within the same painting. But her father is the patriarch who takes centre stage, displaying his art, his certificates, even his work bag, and only after he is finished do Susama and her mother show me their other work and sing together, unfurling a charming painting about a fish wedding.

Her mother, Susama happily says, is the best writer of lyrics.

Her mother tells me that Susama is the best painter in the family.

There is an easy repartee between the two; Susama tells me that it was her mother, Rani, who gave her the idea to draw the first coronavirus scroll, so that doctors could display them in clinics. It is also Rani Chitrakar who is now teaching her sixteen-year-old granddaughter about lyrics and song.

From the time she was five years old, Susama started to draw and sing with her parents. Her grandfather was a painter, and he learned from his forefathers, and so it had been, always, in the family. I look at the children, the daughters huddled together. What about the next generation? The girls?

The eldest daughter, at eighteen, is already an accomplished artist. The next one, at sixteen, is still learning, and the seven-year-old is a beginner.

'What about your son?' I ask. 'Would you prefer him to train for another trade?'

In her answer, Susama emphasizes the words *Bongsher Porompora*—it is a family tradition. Her son will also be an artist. '*Etai amader jibika,*' she says. 'It is our vocation.'

Of course, continues Susama, the pandemic took away their earnings, *kichu chilo na rojkar pati*. She unfurls a scroll and explains it took her eight to ten days to create this one, working day and night. The coronavirus scroll took much longer, and she had made five, but only three sold, one to a buyer in Italy, who commissioned the painting to hang in her medical clinic. The other two sold in Kharagpur and Medinipur, nearby towns she had visited to educate the population about the pandemic.

Usually, Susama's work takes her to large cities—to Mumbai, Bangalore, and Hyderabad—and she has been invited to Delhi many times—for exhibitions at Delhi Haat, Aga Khan Hall, Craft Centre, Sarat Mela—but all this completely stopped, as did the features on TV programmes and YouTube videos. She speaks wistfully of once having travelled to Norway, South Korea, China, and Taiwan, invited to exhibitions to demonstrate her talent to appreciative audiences.

The TV station Zee Bangla helped with donations, and Parvathy Baul, one of the leading Baul musicians in India, donated Rs5,000 (US$62), and the West Bengal government gave Rs1,000 (US$12). They managed. It is getting better now, said Susama, and she would be travelling back with me to Kolkata to deliver some of her paintings to an NGO that markets them. This NGO had been giving them food, soap, sanitizer, and masks, but the monthly income had stopped coming in.

The scrolls are stored away hastily as the paints come out. Patuas use colours from various trees, leaves, flowers, ash, and clay, and the family shows me the metamorphosis of natural elements into vivid hues: chal pora, ash from burned rice, makes black; lakhon phal, soursop dried to powder and mixed with water, gives a deep vermilion; and pui shak, Malabar spinach, is squeezed when ripe for pink; sheem pata, leaves from the sword bean, make green; aparajita phul, the butterfly pea flower, yields blue; theto kore haldi, smashed turmeric, gives a lovely yellow, which grows darker when roasted in the sun; for brown, unoner mati, the mud from the cooking fire, or ground bricks, and unoner chhai, the ash from cooking stoves, is a vivid grey. Colours are mixed together for a more expansive palette. Bel bichi, the seed of the wood apple, is used for glue and is necessary for all the paintings as a shine that lasts without fading.

Susama's father brings out some old scrolls to show me the lasting effects of the paints. The pictures were drawn by his father, long deceased, and the scrolls are faded but colours distinguishable. He tells me they trace an ancestry back to Vishvakarma, the divine craftsman of all weapons for the Gods, for Vishvakarma's youngest son was the first Chitrakar.

I ask them about being Muslim and singing of Hindu Gods, even claiming an ancestry from the Hindu pantheon: do they not receive pushback from the Muslim clerics and Hindu priests?

Rani breaks spontaneously into song:

> *Amra manob jati, ek mayer santan*
> *Keu Hindu bole, keu Mussalman*
> *We are human beings, born of one mother*
> *Some call themselves Hindu, some Muslim*

She unscrolls a painting of the demolition of the Babri Masjid in 1992, India aflame with sectarian violence. Her response had been to sing of unity and brotherhood.

Historically, the Chitrakar community has been ostracized by both Muslim and Hindu societies because their artistic repertoire has included Hindu hymns, specifically the *Manasa Mangal, Chandi Mangal,* and *Lokkhi Broto* in praise of Hindu Goddesses, leading to a backlash from Brahminical fanatics as well as Muslim clergy.

In the current age of Hindutva politics in India, has this situation worsened? On our drive back to Kolkata, Susama and her husband deny facing any problems. Kolkata, they say, is not like North India.

Their community is strictly endogamous, and as they discuss an upcoming wedding, it is clear that there are schisms even within their community, and they bicker gently about the bride's community, their stature, their differences. It is a private conversation I don't want to eavesdrop on, so I delight in the smooth ride back to Kolkata, the highway wide and with decent restaurants along the way. Susama says it is all due to West Bengal's chief minister, Mamata Banerjee, whom they all refer to fondly as Didi. Banerjee has schemes for the well-being of young girls, meals in schools, scholarships for disadvantaged students. For artisans, the government pays Rs1,000 per artisan, per month, so a family of four gets Rs4,000 (US$50) per month, enough to make room for creating art without worrying about feeding the family.

Susama's family is one among the many in Pingla keeping alive an ancient art form of India and tackling social issues in a way that can be understood by some of the poorest and most marginalized populations in our world, people with limited access to electricity or smartphones. More than religious divides, it is perhaps the globalization of India that is the biggest threat to this art form; how can a Patua artist like Susama, with a painted paper scroll and a song on her lips, compete with the streaming services providing nonstop entertainment on television or the Bollywood extravaganza with CGI graphics enhancing storytelling?

I hope they prevail, families like Susama's, who for generations, have lived within the marginal but undoubtedly secure place in West Bengal society. The modern world may be challenging some certainties, but it has also opened up the possibilities of social media and YouTube channels as well as travel abroad, and it is clear that Patuas like Susama are resilient and determined to claim their place in modern India. This small family, all practising artists or active apprentices, is committed to keeping their Bongsher Porompora—a family tradition—very much alive.

Bollywood Dancing in the Netherlands

It is past seven in the evening in a community centre in Daalwijkdreef, in Amsterdam. Cars are jammed into the tiny parking lot; some are double-parked. Inside, a female singer is belting out loud raunchy lyrics through a CD:

> *Na gilaf, na lihaf, thandi hawa bhi khilaf sasurree!* . . .
> *No blanket, no quilt, the freezing wind is a bitch!* . . .
> *Bidi Jalaile Jigar Se Piya, Jigar Maa Badi Aag Hain* . . .
> *Light your cigarette with my heart beloved, I'm on fire* . . .

The song, titled *Bidi Jalaile*, is from the Bollywood movie *Omkara* (2006). This is a rustic, suggestive song which was featured as an 'item-number' in Bollywood parlance, which means that the dance is very sexy. The fourteen women in the room are writhing to the beat with abandon. Most are mouthing the lyrics; the movie was filmed in a UP dialect of Hindi, similar to the Bhojpuri that the Surinamese-Hindustanis speak.

I am observing these women, as well as participating in the Bollywood dancing class as the singularly Most Untalented Member. How the language identities evolve for women in the Surinamese-Hindustani community, and how their roles play out in the larger Dutch society has been the focus of my sociolinguistic research, and will continue to hold my attention for fourteen months at the International Institute of Asian Studies, in Leiden, the Netherlands from 2007–2009.

* * *

Leiden is an old and erudite city filled with wall poems in many languages. The poem painted on the wall outside my office ends with *There's no time. Or is there nothing but time?*

This is an ancient town that looks exactly the same in the paintings from the seventeenth and eighteenth centuries that hang in the museums. It is a city so impossibly beautiful that it spoils you for other places. The Kern Library, a haven for Indophiles, has iron trellised staircases leading to a maze of books, the books bordered by ancient Tibetan tankhas displayed on the walls.

My office at the Nonnensteeg, where nuns once prayed, is an oasis of tranquillity in the middle of a botanical garden. One window looked down into a narrow alley so picturesque that I had to research whether it was the same alley in Vermeer's famous painting (it wasn't).

* * *

The Surinamese-Hindustani community is positioned within a multilingual Europe, within a continent still coming to terms with the racial tensions inherent in a multilingual population with cultural pluralism. Approximately 160,000 Hindustanis, the Indo-Surinamese, live in the Netherlands and hold Dutch citizenship and I was focusing on women of this community to specifically study language maintenance and loss. The Surinamese-Hindustani community is a diaspora of 'twice-migrants'. Most are descended from indentured labour recruited to work in Suriname; on 5 June 1873, the first ship

Lalla Rookh arrived at Paramaribo after a three-month voyage from Calcutta, carrying 452 labourers, mostly recruited from the states known as Uttar Pradesh and Bihar today.[5] Prior to the Independence of Suriname from the Netherlands in 1975, and driven by the threat of the same kind of ethnic violence that characterized the independence of other Caribbean nations, many of the Surinamese-Hindustanis migrated to the Netherlands. In June 2008, the community celebrated 135 years of their immigration history with cultural shows and scholarly speeches in Den Hague, much of it celebrating the fact that the children of labourers were now a model minority in their new homeland.

Bollywood blockbusters like *Silsila* and *Hum Tum* have been shot in the Netherlands, and there even is a tulip named after the reigning queen of Bollywood, Aishwarya Rai. Indiawijzer.nl listed twelve different Bollywood dance institutes scattered all over the Netherlands. There was also a growing interest by mainstream Dutch audiences; the dance instructor mentioned a growing demand for the shows he choreographed for the Holland Casino and the classes at the Kunst Akademie, attended by non-Indian students. The instructor had spent time as a back-up dancer in Bollywood, and was equally at home with salsa, meringue and even belly dancing.

The Daalwijkdreef area of Amsterdam had a large migrant population, and was dense with people, the laundry spilling over narrow balconies. Our class met every Wednesday for an hour, from 6.00–7.00 in the evening, and the women ranged in age from late twenties to late forties, and there was a strong

---

[5] Mukherjee, Dipika, 'Loving Bollywood and Being Dutch: Multilingual code-switching and Identity issues among Surinamese-Indian women in Amsterdam.' In Dubois, I, Baumgartner N (eds). *Multilingual Identities: New Global Perspectives*. Frankfurt am Main: Peter Lang, 87–97, 2013.

sense of community as the women enrolled in this class had friends or relatives who took lessons in Bollywood dancing (usually daughters and/or sisters). Few came alone. There were no 'divas' in this class, unlike the teenagers' class which met an hour earlier and was teasingly titled the Little Angels.

Religion did not come up until I interviewed the participants individually, and then I discovered that this class had Muslim, Hindu and Christian women from the Surinamese-Hindustani community. At least four languages are spoken in the daily lives of the members of the Surinamese-Hindustani community in the Netherlands, and they are: Sarnami Hindi, Dutch, Standard Hindi and Sranan Tongo. Sarnami Hindi was the main language of communication within the Hindustani community and within Hindustani families.

However, Dutch was clearly the language of communication in this class. There was some singing along in Hindi, as well as the instructor's encouraging *Kya Baat Hai!* (Good Job!) comments, but the language of instruction was in Dutch.

Although there was a basic understanding of standard Hindi among all participants in the Bollywood Dance class, the fluency varied. Interestingly, there was some confusion about the nomenclature of the language used; participants were unwilling to label it as Hindi, Bhojpuri, Sarnami or anything else; most chose to call the language 'our Hindi'.

In this community, the women were insistent about the need to teach their children their own language:

> Also my Hindi for my children . . . I'm proud to be a Hindustani and I want them also proud to be a Hindustani, also in Netherlands, I want them to live here, invite people, but not forget their own culture and their own traditions. When I'm walking in Holland, I'm on the street, I'm looking at an old Indian woman ask me something, I'm so proud I can talk to her in Hindi.

In this age of global deracination, a sense of belonging can be completely unrelated to any essentialist notion of geophysical space. The women in this community spoke of a sense of feeling Hindustani, but no connection with India as a nation. During the interviews with the participants, home was *never* India; India was associated with poverty, and being 'crowdy'.

Home was not the Netherlands either; place of birth as well as age at migration was a strong predictor of attitude. The younger the person was at the age of migration, the stronger the ties with the Netherlands. However, the women in my study came to the Netherlands as teenagers or adults and frequently self-identified as 'Hindustani' over the other possible categories 'Dutch' or 'Indian'.

Suriname was presented as a community idyll in many of the stories I heard. One spoke of a mother-in-law's recovery from a deadly disease once she returned to Suriname and another told me her story of the community celebrating the Muslim tradition of Qurbani as one family, no matter how large. There was both regret and loss in these stories.

The Surinamese-Hindustani women in the Netherlands were conflicted by their own sense of who they are and what they can become, especially when faced with the contradictory forces of living within the very liberal cities of this country. There are many areas in which the women's aspirations and self-image did not mesh with that that expected by the Surinamese-Hindustani community.

This made the community prone to a very high suicide rate, with women between the ages of fifteen and twenty-four being at the highest risk. The problem was not minor, with girls from the community choosing suicide at rates almost triple the Dutch national average.

The conflicts the women faced started with societal norms on how females were valued and the emphasis placed on chastity and marriage. There was the taboo of exogamous marriage and many constraints on women's movements. The pressures on women were more oppressive than on their brothers, leading to despair.

The women shared their stories of suicide in the community, some quite harrowing. The good news was that once the women survived past the age of twenty-five, they often became mentors for the teenagers and women in their early twenties, spotting the signs of distress and acting quickly.

These women were survivors. There was much to be learnt from a sorority such as this, with its sense of sisterhood and solidarity that crossed religious and cultural barriers. Bollywood was the most accessible means for language retention of a familiar tongue, but what was most intriguing was the specific ways in which this group created their own ways of speaking and thereby redefined their place in the larger Indian diaspora.

* * *

The Dutch are a pragmatic race, easy to work with, and with no affectations. The phrase that defined the country was *doe maar gewoon, dan doe je al gek genoeg* which is an admonition for 'just act normal, it's already crazy enough'.

This is a very picturesque part of the world, with perfect views of soaring spires and ancient churches at almost every turn of a canal. However, a large number of these churches are no longer houses for worship, but event spaces.

In Maastricht, I stopped at the world's finest bookstore located inside a fabulous old Dominican church, dating from the thirteenth century. Built in 1294, the cathedral now soars above the three-storied bookstore, with plenty of open spaces for readers to browse, with a café in the corner.

Converting this rarely-used church into a bookstore may have seemed heretical to some, but it is such a sensible idea. When Maastricht was invaded by Napoleon in 1794 and the Dominicans forced out of the country, the church had been briefly used as a parish, but then fell into neglect as a warehouse, an archive, and finally a giant parking lot for bicycles. The bookstore's thoughtful renovation of an ancient space gave the awe-inspiring fourteenth century ceiling frescoes a new lease of life.

Similarly, the new Asian Library at the University of Leiden had an official opening in the iconic Pieterskerk of Leiden, and Queen Máxima, as the patroness of the Royal Netherlands Institute of Southeast Asian and Caribbean Studies (KITLV), presided over the opening ceremony at this late-Gothic church in Leiden dedicated to Saint Peter. The history of this church can be traced back to 1100. Pieterskerk is also known as the church of the Pilgrim Fathers, for the early European settlers of what is now Plymouth, in Massachusetts, had fled England for the relative tolerance of sixteenth- to seventeenth-century Holland, and then continued to North America, where they established a colony in 1620.

However, Pieterskerk wears its long history lightly and now largely functions as a space for university and community events. Leiden University was founded in 1575 and has several ancient buildings within its own campus, but choosing this ancient church for the inaugural event gave the occasion an added gravitas. Within Pieterskerk, in this grand space dating back to 1100, under the vaulted ceilings and lush lighting, the Queen and the audience listened to speeches about the importance of libraries and international collaborative research, from the time of the Silk Routes and beyond.

I published a book with the Amsterdam University Press, and was delighted to see the office in Amsterdam had stained-glass windows celebrating reading and music in the way that churches once deified saints and messiahs. Many ancient civilizations—including the Chinese, Indian, Norse, Japanese, Persian, Armenian, Mongols, Egyptians—had deities of knowledge. Perhaps we should all venerate the search for knowledge in the same way we venerate our religious convictions.

In the Netherlands, among the Surinamese-Hindustani sorority and within churches as spaces that honoured knowledge, the world just seems like a kinder, wiser place.

Tears and Song

This will be my first Father's Day in the US without my father. Papa did not die of COVID, but he took his last breath in Delhi, at a time when the city was deep in pandemic hell.

When I answered a panicked phone call in Chicago, ten days before Papa passed away, I was already vaccinated with two doses of the Pfizer BioNTech vaccine, and had started to resume a normal life as cafes and outdoor events started to open up in this beautiful city I call home. I had been following what was happening in India—most of my family lives in Delhi, and I have numerous relatives in West Bengal—and it was déjà vu of the worst kind, as the news reports took me back to a year ago, when New York was the epicentre of COVID mismanagement in the US, and the federal government refused to take any responsibility.

Hospitals in Delhi had no beds, so we decided to keep Papa, ninety-four, at home. When he first showed signs of a stroke on 25 April, words as mumbled verbiage, his language shifted entirely from Bengali to English. As a career diplomat he was fluent in English, but our home language is uncompromisingly Bengali, so it shook my brother, Dada, when my father who had long expressed a wish to live to be a hundred years old, the father who said he would not die until he saw my invalid brother, Amit, sitting up and feeding himself, whispered clearly and resolutely in English, 'I'm dying, I'm dying.'

Medical staff all over India were already choosing who to save and who to sacrifice, and a man of ninety-four years had no chance in the second wave targeting younger people. In Delhi alone, the toll of patients aged sixty and over declined from 62 per cent in January 2021 to 52 per cent in April 2021, but numbers for those aged 49–59 rose to 32 per cent of all deaths. The mortality rate of those aged 18–44 was at 18 per cent and rising, and understandably, this was the population that hospital staff thought had the best chance of recovery, and received the most care from hospital staff.

Papa passed away on 8 May 2021 at 9.15 a.m.; that is the time/date stamp on the Death Certificate. But he probably breathed his last as early as just after 11 p.m., on 7 May, after he stopped breathing through the nebulizer mask. We were privileged to have full-time nursing care for my eldest brother, bedridden after a cycling accident, and it was this night nurse who worked vigorously on his chest as we looked on in confusion. We continued to get a faint pulse even after that, and the oxygen saturation remained at levels that showed him to be alive. But rigor mortis started to set in, his skin turning lighter and lighter, and we turned the air-conditioning to twenty-two degrees Celsius to prevent the ravages of the Delhi summer outside from affecting my father's growingly rigid body.

No doctor was available to visit the house, so we had to wait. Wait through the night, no longer sure whether my father had passed on or could hear us. My mother has no memory of that night. She went to sleep in another room, confused by the confusion in us all, unwilling to accept the loss of the companion of well over half a century.

Without a death certificate there could be no cremation. And while we continued to imagine a faint pulsebeat, there would be no cremation.

At about 6.30 that morning, with no doctor available to attend to my father's cold body, I started to wonder whether the decision to keep Papa at home had been a mistake.

* * *

In Delhi, not only did Prime Minister Narendra Modi deflect all blame for the mismanagement of this crisis, the government embarked on a $2.8 billion vanity project, desecrating the historical parts of Lutyen's Delhi, and in a clear statement dishonouring anything living, began to uproot heritage trees nearly 100 years old. Anish Kapoor, creator of Chicago's iconic 'Bean' installed in the Millenium Park, called Modi's destruction of Delhi architecture the act of a Hindu Taliban.

In Chicago, I had taken the RT-PCR test required to fly into India, and reached New Delhi on a direct flight from O'Hare to Indira Gandhi International Airport with few travellers. Delhi streets felt abandoned. But life at home seemed normal; on the night I reached Delhi, my father had dinner seated at the dining table. In Indian homes, at arrivals and departures, we touch the feet of our elders, for ashirbaad—which can only be translated into English as a blessing, but it is deeply imbued with a generational tenderness, the older ensuring the longevity and happiness of the younger, and my father placed his hand on my head in that heartfelt gesture, welcoming me home.

My scholarly father taught me early that aashirbaad is like knowledge, something that increases when it is freely spent and destroyed if unshared with others. In his final days, he would seek out my face, his uncoordinated fingers pecking at my forehead like a blind bird feeding its young.

Medical care at home is affordable and excellent in India; we already knew this because my eldest brother was being cared for at home. Doctors in India still make home visits, and our family physician is Dr D. Dhar, whose physician father had attended to mine. The young Dr Dhar could be counted upon to attend to medical emergencies at our home, even in the middle of the night. Until the pandemic changed our certainties.

Dr Dhar's clinic is a modest establishment with one person managing the office. It makes no attempt to compete with the swanky medical institutions or mega-hospitals of South Delhi. Yet Dr Dhar was so inundated by the patients in his clinic that he stopped answering phone calls, or even responding to our frantic texts.

* * *

Three days after I arrived, Papa started to lose the ability to control his body. He had to be fed, with a teaspoon, then a large syringe pushing gruel into his mouth, and was rapidly losing strength. I tried feeding him ground-up medicine through a syringe but it must have tasted so awful that he spat out the mixture immediately.

Dada took over the task of feeding him, gently coaxing his mouth to open. One of the most beautiful images I have from this time—forever embedded in only my mind —is of Papa holding Dada's shoulder to stay propped up, like a small child, and looking deep into Dada's eyes as he accepted another spoonful of food, his eyes filled with trust so absolute that I had to blink away my tears.

The nurse who has been attending to my vegetative brother at home for the past five years is a Muslim man named Nafeez. Nafeez has become a member of my family; I mention his religion as important to our story, as this is the new India that I am fiercely proud of. My traditional paternal grandmother had been widowed during the Partition of India and had scraped a living in a village outside Calcutta with seven mouths to feed;

anti-Muslim sentiment ran high in my ancestral home, where non-Brahmins were barely tolerated and Muslims not at all. Yet Nafeez came into our lives in 2016 and became so much a part of the family that he shared the food we ate. He was Papa's companion through many nights, as my insomniac father roamed the rooms, often flipping through his beloved books, but most often just looking for conversation.

It was Nafeez who said that if Papa was not put on some sort of intravenous drips, he would soon starve to death. While Dada hovered over Papa, I stood at Dr Dhar's clinic, late at night, in an attempt to force him to come home with me, no matter how late the hour. My brother needed his tracheostomy tube changed, and Papa's condition was deteriorating, so we had two developing emergencies at home.

At a quarter to midnight, when it was finally my turn to see the doctor, there were still fourteen more patients waiting their turn. Dr Dhar is a youthful man, light of gait, but on that day, his eyes behind the face shield and mask were weary. There was no time for niceties. When I told him of the situation at home, he gave me a Sophies Choice: 'Pick one,' he said in a voice filled with exhaustion, 'I can only see any ONE of your patients.'

I burst into tears. 'Papa,' I mumbled. 'Please. Papa is dying.'

* * *

Dr Dhar's visit confirmed what we had all begun to understand by then. This time, there would be no pulling Papa back from the brink. Papa needed palliative care. His hands moved in agitated parabolas towards his head, scratching at his scalp in an attempt to soothe the insides, his face contorted. We took to holding his hands, running our fingers through his hair.

I sang Rabindra Sangeet. Tagore's poetry rendered into song is the soundtrack of most Bengali households, and I sang my father's favourites, badly and voice breaking, about our astonishment at this vast universe, and the miracle of our place in it. I sang the songs that I would sing to my young boys as a lullaby, of birds in the trees, *kuhu, kuhu, kuhu gaye*, the Delhi evenings bursting into actual birdsong as my father became a child, lulled into a gentle, peaceful sleep. My mother held my father's hand, my brother snuggled at his feet.

Before my father stopped breathing, we had put him on oxygen, but cylinders were notoriously hard to buy or refill. On the night of 7 May, Dada and I were frantically calling the twenty-four-hour hotlines set up by grassroots organizations, and it was the Sikh Gurdwaras that answered our calls, even after midnight. The waiting line for oxygen cylinders were at least three hours long.

Nafeez found a distributor selling cylinders at the black-market rate of Rs20,000 per cylinder, but we would have to cross the Delhi border to secure one, a difficult, if not impossible, feat in a lockdown. There was no guarantee that we wouldn't be delayed by road blocks and arrive too late for the cylinder to be of any use.

I had seen the news reports about bodies washing up on riverbeds, the lines at crematoriums, the unceasing obituaries of the dead. But for the first time that night, I realized the helpless panic of families caring for a dying person. I saw how, in the absence of government leadership, the grassroots organizations, often religious groups, stepped in to help anyone in need. It shouldn't have been this hard.

It was a community of doctors in J-Block of Chittaranjan Park that sent one of their own to certify Papa's passing. This community also helped us search for oxygen cylinders through the night. The final message on my phone from them is a message of condolence, regretting their inability to do more to keep my father alive.

* * *

To honour my father, I will go to the Art Institute of Chicago, and stand at the entrance of Fullerton Hall, and read the writing in Bengali. The plaque commemorates the visit of Swami Vivekananda on 11 September 1893, to speak in front of an audience of seven thousand people who had gathered for the Parliament of the World's Religions. The picture is of a young Vivekanda, just thirty years old, arms crossed and looking to the side, posing for the camera. On top, in large letters, are the words in cursive 'Sisters and Brothers of America'.

What has become a legend in Bengali families like mine, is that the moment Swami Vivekananda launched his speech introducing Hinduism and Vedanta to a Western audience, he began with the words 'Sisters and Brothers of America', a departure from the formal 'Ladies and Gentlemen' and his reference to a universal kinship that binds us all resulted in a deafening applause, which lasted a full two minutes. I suspected the story to be apocryphal, until I read Swami Vivekananda describing the moment in his own words:

> In my first speech in this country, in Chicago, I addressed that audience as 'Sisters and Brothers of America', and you know that they all rose to their feet. You may wonder what made them do this, you may wonder if I had some strange power.

My father gave me a lifelong love for words; for memorizing poetry and speeches that feed the soul; a rooted home in black-in-white in this unrooted world. A world I could always turn to, one that would offer solace and privacy and be truly mine. I grew up with stories of Vivekananda, and other people who changed the world with words.

And through all this, the most important gift he gave me was the strong foundation of belief in my own talent. When I was twelve, in New Zealand, and had performed a solo at a

Bharatnatyam dance recital, Papa would write to relatives, and even say this conversationally, that the audience had stood up and clapped, a standing ovation like that given to Vivekananda when he delivered an iconic sermon at the World's Congress of Religions in Chicago in 1893, knowing well that I would understand the heft of this comparison.

May more fathers—in India and around the world—convince their daughters that when they pursue a talent, the world will give them a standing ovation.

Of course, the Vivekananda simile was wildly overblown, compared to my own achievements. Yet when Chicago became home, and Papa's memory was fading and he would not remember where I was calling from, I would just say *Chicago* and he would launch into *Brothers and Sisters*, his voice shaky with the delight of oratory. And I would visit the Art Institute of Chicago and stand at the entrance of Fullerton Hall where Vivekananda's speech is commemorated in Bengali and English. At these times, Chicago felt like a warm fatherly embrace, even if my father was miles away.

Musings

Paet Puja

Port Dickson. Sea breeze off the Malacca Straits, the sun sliding reluctantly into the pool of night. This may be a resort haven for all Malaysians, but in November, it becomes a place of pilgrimage for the Malaysian Bengalis.

We drive for miles on the long public holiday of Deepavali, coming from as far away as Penang and Singapore, and as near as Seremban. We gather at Pujo Bari for the worship of the Goddess Kali, but as Bengalis are often the first to ruefully admit, our paet pujo—worship of our stomachs—triumphs much else. Pujo Bari, for two magical days, becomes the diaspora's Mecca for communal comfort food.

Pujo Bari looks old and dates from the 1950s; it is a once-decrepit colonial bungalow bought by collecting a half-month salary from the long-deceased forefathers of the present generation. It was an extraordinary generation that colluded so selflessly to ensure a community heritage for us all, and the ties to what we consider ancestral property still run deep. It no longer matters whether we are related by blood to the others, or how modern we are, and whether our education or marriage makes us speak in different tongues. Ultimately, we are all still Bengali. We all understand, through a deep collective unconscious that makes our tongues salivate—jibhe jol ashe— that Pujo Bari food is the best in the world.

Deepavali for us means two days and one sleepless night of homage to the Goddess Kali, the one who obliterates ignorance and fear and evil while celebrating the joys of life. And what an uninhibited celebration it is, including meat and alcohol, for food is a big component of Kali Puja.

The true Pujo Bari experience begins before the official festivities start, with the first convoy of cars trundling down the highway and into the Pujo Bari compound. Mutthamma, the mother of the present caretaker, made the best egg curry in all of Malaysia on this planet and it was Mutthamma's Mutta Curry, a fragrant dish of eggs in a spicy ginger-cumin-tomato base, that would fill our hearts and tummies after the long drive. This alliterative marvel tripped off our tongues and brought us all straight here, silencing the children who hankered for the fried chicken and mee goreng at the highway rest-stops, for there was no stopping for makan anywhere else—*hurry up lah, Mutthamma's Mutta Curry may finish if we are late.*

Yet it was a divinely simple dish of eggs and potatoes floating in fragrant gold, easy to add eggs to when the crowds swelled to larger than normal, especially as the chickens roamed free in a compound where the yapping dogs were tied up and the monkeys swung from the trees in the forest beyond.

Mutthamma is no more, but her Mutta Curry recipe lives on. Every year, lunch is still mutta curry and a simple dal. The meal is barely over before the trestle tables are brought out and set up in preparation for dinner. Ancient botis, with curved knives held by the foot so that both hands are free to cut precisely, are taken out. The younger chefs, unable to sit on the ground and manipulate botis, stand with Japanese knives at the ancient table trembling under the weight of beans and potatoes and cauliflower and lentils . . .

. . . and, of course, meat.

No Kali Puja is complete without goat meat, and in Bengal, it was once traditional for young goats to be sacrificed at the altar of the Goddess. Such animal sacrifice is now frowned upon as primitive, so a pumpkin is theatrically sliced, in time to the ceremonial drumming of gongs and ringing of bells and the sonorous long wail of the conch shell. Women ululate while the priest chants mantras. Then the pumpkin 'sacrifice'—boli—is mixed with the raw goat meat sweating in a spicy marinade, and brought into the kitchen. More chilli-turmeric-salt-coriander-cumin mix is added, then the concoction is left to be cooked with large dollops of dry garam masala spices, the masalas making the spice-mix passed as a heritage through the generations.

Cooking for the community used to be something a man would do, through the 50s and the 60s and the 70s. Women have almost completely taken over the reins in recent years, but the helpers are invariably male, and they stand by to stir the large vats of bubbling broth, oaring through the mix with ladles in synchronicity under the sharp gaze of the mashis, who watch to make sure the cloves and star anise are not blackened, then ladle out the cinnamon and indicate when to sprinkle some extra ghee.

Today, the food is still cooked over large open clay stoves. Dishes are washed in a large free-standing antique bathtub. Huge kualis still clang with the sound of large spatulas as gargantuan proportions of spices and condiments are stirred into the bubbling mix—surely, the turmeric is too much, the salt too generous?—but then the smells, miraculously, punctuate the air with the promise of perfection.

There is another kitchen—the pure one—where the group that fasts through the night of Kali Puja, not allowing a drop of water to pass their lips, prepares the offering for the Goddess. Here, everything is fried in the purest ghee, the rice is the best basmati, and the dried fruits are of premium quality. Everyone bathes before stepping into the inner sanctum; there is no onion, no garlic, and everything is opened from containers that have been freshly bought, not even tainted by refrigeration. The vessels gleam copper and steel, some new, some antique, all scrupulously cleaned for divine offerings. The cooks in this temple taste nothing, yet this food must be the best if it is to be offered to a Goddess known for a temper so fierce that she danced around the world in a rage of destruction until her husband, Shiva, lay down on her path.

The prayer hall kitchen is adjacent to the open kitchen, and the sizzling cumin and the smoking ghee smells mingle, despite the hibiscus trees that line the periphery. But no one minds, especially not the Goddess, who smiles benevolently towards the open bar.

Yes, there is—always—alcohol at Kali Puja.

The young ask for rum mixed into Coke or a splash of gin in Sprite; an older cousin acting as the bartender is happy to do the mixing. The older enterprising menfolk start a car-o-bar from the boot of a Mercedes parked under the angsana tree, tippling back neat single malts while keeping an eye on the children who are letting off the firecrackers too close to the precious premium vehicles.

In the main kitchen, slices of carp are dusted with turmeric, salt and chilli powder. The fish is lightly seared on both sides—too much and it will be rubbery—and then transferred into a kuali where potatoes and cauliflower bubble, tempered with nigella seeds and cumin-coriander powder. The fish is stirred very gently, as making the perfect *macher jhol*—the quintessential Bengali fish stew—is a matter of expertise. Brides were once chosen for their ability to crisp without breakage the small sweet river fish of the Bengali delta, and there is still nothing in the modern kitchen that is nearly as daunting to master.

A sizzle of vegetables is fried up in two kualis as the afternoon starts darkening into the evening. There is always *bhaja,* a combination of paper-thin brinjals, pointed gourd, okra and cauliflower, the edges fried crunchy-crisp. This is served with *narkol diye chholar dal*—Bengal gram boiled into a mushy comfort food, then tempered with asafoetida and cinnamon-cloves, then a sprinkle of sugar with sizzling cumin seeds and the merest hint of dried red chillies. Just before serving, it is infused with small squares of fresh-fried coconut and ladled out steaming hot . . . just the smell of this is pure heaven.

It is a sweaty job, cooking in the open tropical kitchen, and the chefs disperse to rest and change into iridescent clothes for the all-night festivities.

The crowd swells again as the night deepens into violet hues, and the sky lights up with the iridescence of a hundred firecrackers set off in unison. Someone starts humming a tune, the refrain of which is picked up by the group, and another starts to drum on the wooden table as another scurries off to overturn a nearby bucket to fashion into a deep tabla thrum. There is much laughter and jollity over misheard or misremembered Rabindra Sangeet lyrics—and in this group—mispronunciations.

It is a joyous cacophony of sound that lasts all night. Women in gorgeous silk saris gather outside the altar of the Goddess to thinly slice watermelon chunks and pears and apples and mangoes and persimmons and pomegranates into a mix for the prasad. There is the unpeeling of bananas, to be mixed with curd and sweets, and sprinkled with nuts. A group of young women kneel on the floor, carefully arranging 108 brass oil lamps, then slowly lighting them without singeing their arms. The air is heavy with the scent of jasmine and roses and sandalwood incense.

There is a cultural programme, then the mad rush for the buffet-style dinner. A genteel allowance is made for older seniors; the kinship ties are not of blood, but rooted in the heart. Plates are ladled with food and the round tables animated by the conversation. The same green plates and glasses, the forks with tines missing and spoons out of shape are bent into usage. Someone makes sure the food—especially the meat and fish— are placed behind the netted meat-safe for the fasting group to eat later.

An abundance of sweets—rosogolla and sandesh and langcha—made by the mishti experts at home is brought in refrigerated boxes. If we are lucky, there may even be labongo lotika, a notoriously time-consuming pastry to make, with sweet flour, khoya and ghee, sealed with a clove to hold down the centre.

There is always enough food, usually too much. So much so that we are exhorted into eating souring curries and stale rice before our long drives back, a decision which will force some of us to take more rest stops than we intended. But it is pujo bari food, cooked with love, and we return to eat seconds, and then eat again. Usually, just as dawn is breaking and the sun is setting the sea alight with the first drizzle of fire, the priest and the fasting devotees gather to eat their first taste of non-vegetarian food in twenty-four hours. Some of us will join them again for yet another meal.

There is always room here and we find another plastic stool to be drawn into the inner circle. Everyone is welcome as we eat spicy mutton with rice, the crisp pop of a green chilly in hand to bite, and end with sweet curd to sweeten the mouth.

There is the sweet and the spicy, the salty and the crisp, the mushy and the fragrant. It is a perfect Malaysian meal for the multitudes we embrace, holding on to the ancient while navigating our new worlds.

Glocal Voices

In 2002, Kirpal Singh, Mohammad Quayum, and I co-edited *The Merlion and the Hibiscus: Contemporary Short Stories from Singapore and Malaysia*, an anthology published by Penguin Books. This book was explicitly designed to present Malaysian and Singapore voices to an international audience and was largely a labour of love; books of short stories don't sell, and fifteen years ago, before names such as Jhumpa Lahiri and Munro won prizes like the Pulitzer and Nobel, anthologies were a hard sell indeed. Plus, we were trying to publish short stories from a region where writers writing in English were highly suspect as post-colonial pretenders with colonialist souls.

Few writers from Southeast Asia reached an international audience then, but this book, because of the marketing arm of Penguin Books, was reviewed in publications from Hong Kong to India. Whereas Malaysian and Singaporean newspapers treated the project with nationalistic fervour and announced 'Literary voices for export' and (perplexingly) 'Yes, Size Does Matter', a reviewer from India pointed to a certain thematic bravery:

> Is 'multiculturalism' really as disinterested and neutral as it seems to be, or does it have its own silences, its own propensity to become part of certain hegemonies? These are questions that must be asked.
>
> —*The Statesman*, 21 April 2002

As editors, our biggest slap on the wrist came from a reviewer from Hong Kong, who wrote:

> Absent for the most part are the heavy political themes of freedom and religious tolerance that often dominate coffee shop conversations.
>
> —*Far Eastern Economic Review*, 4 July 2002

Wonderful. So we had produced a timid and polite little collection that had little sound and even less fury. The stories were well-crafted and written by the leading lights of the region in 2002, but unlike the South American writers who were mining gold with magic realism retelling stories about sociocultural upheavals in their countries, our anthology largely left taboo topics alone.

In 2018, I co-edited my fifth anthology of Malaysian English writing, *Endings and Beginnings,* with Sharon Bakar. This anthology grew out of prize-winning and publishable entries from the D.K. Dutt Award for Literary Excellence, which was established in 2015 as an annual contest to foster new Malaysian voices.

From 2002 to the latest anthology in 2018, one would expect changes; but has anything really changed in the zeitgeist of Malaysian English writing in a decade and a half?

Yes. And No.

Self-censorship continues to foster a certain timidity in regional writing. Of course, the self-censorship is not without cause; *The Merlion and the Hibiscus* was held up in customs in Johor Bahru for a week as the officers decided whether the homosexual story in this volume was 'safe' for Malaysian consumption. During the editing of *The Merlion and the Hibiscus*, a young man in his early twenties withdrew a story about wrestling with his sexual identity from this collection. 'I'm Malay, lah', he said, in the way of explanation, 'They'll think the whole community is like that only.'

Unfortunately, identity politics, and how writers choose to write about fluid sexual identities, still plague Malaysian writing. While bemoaning the state of literature in the region and the paucity of good writers, there is still a numbing self-censorship that makes authors draw back from the precipice before they got too near. To be a writer in Malaysia while steering clear of politics and ideology, religion and language, one is reminded of Jane Austen's 'the little bit (two inches wide) of Ivory on which I work with so fine a brush, as produces little effect after much labour.'

When I published my debut novel, I too tussled with the demons of self-censorship—*Will it be banned? Do I have the authority to write this book?* A book on the sociopolitical realities of Malaysia, this novel opened with a model being blown to shreds in a field in Shah Alam. I continue to get questions about the imaginative leaps in this work, for this story is rooted in toyols and bolster ghosts, as well as the Brahma-Saraswati lore, brought to life by snippets from news reports. I continue to explain—to largely Western audiences—that I simply dived into the cornucopia of local fables and there is an abundance still untapped in Malaysia.

Ever since Vikram Chandra wrote a seminal article about *The Cult of Authenticity* in 2000, writers have been wary of peddling a country's exoticism—the perils of peddling one's ethnicity, really—as a widely successful multigenerational migrant saga that sells so well in English-speaking markets but says nothing to the region it sprouts from. Fixi, a leading Malaysian indie publisher, wittily warned against irrelevance in a manifesto to all new writers seeking publication under their imprint: 'We publish stories about the urban reality of Malaysia. If you want to share your grandmother's World War II stories, send 'em elsewhere and you might even win the Booker Prize.'

In the past two decades, the world has opened up for Malaysian glocal writers, those writing globally while rooted firmly in local sensibilities. Some remain resident in Malaysia: Writers such as Hanna Alkaf, who takes on mental illness and 13 May in one breathtaking Malaysian YA novel, *The Weight of Our Sky*; Writers like Brian Gomez who can write *A Devil's Place* as a brilliant urban KL noir; Preeta Samasaran and Bernice Chauly rewriting the family saga as domestic and sociopolitical unrest; Zen Cho playing with dystopian worlds with Malaysian flavours; Yangsze Choo taking *The Ghost Bride* to Netflix fame, right on the heels of the phenomenal Hollywood success of *Crazy Rich Asians*. In 2022, two important books pushing the boundaries were published: Preeta Samarasan's *Tale of a Dreamer's Son* and *The Accidental Malay* by Karina Robles Bahrin, both intrepid in addressing religion and identity politics in modern Malaysia.

At the Georgetown Literary Festival (GTLF) in November 2018, Malaysian writers addressed sexuality and politics through inspirational poetry jams and midnight live storytelling sessions that frizzled with promise and engagement. Stories coming out of Malaysia take more chances now. Writing the Malaysian migrant story has moved on to writers such as Raidah Shah Idil and Marc de Faoite, rooted in Malaysia but circumnavigating the globe for a place in the world to forge relationships familial and communal, whether in Malaysia or Ireland or Australia. Sharmilla Ganesan rewrites Southeast Asian myths and fables with gorgeous resonance, and Saras Manickam is a writer to watch. The GTLF remains an international festival to watch, although the 2022 version was a tamer version of pre-COVID times, especially as a new government in Malaysia had brought in more hope instead of active resistance.

GTLF takes place in Penang, and feels like an older, freer Malaysia. There are honest and open discussions; and even the politicians inaugurating the festival seem perilously outspoken. There is a space open here for multiplicity and multilingualism in a way that feels very different from the severity of Kuala Lumpur.

I will close with a quote from Rehman Rashid, a friend and colleague who wrote in his book, *A Malaysian Journey*:

> . . . Malaysia was a hopeless mess of conflicting priorities, mutually unintelligible languages, contradictory cultures and blinkered religions. Malaysia's politics were divisive, its economy exploitative, its pillars of authority buttressed by an impenetrable scaffolding of draconian laws upheld by a parliament in which dominance seemed to matter far more than debate. There was no reason for Malaysia to have survived this far . . . But Malaysia had.

And Malaysian writers will too—as long as they continue to confront and challenge the gritty realities of Malaysia—they will not only survive, but also prosper. There is a wealth of talent in this region that is just beginning to find their global, intrepid voices.

Do My Poems Cry with Me?

Rarely is poetry, with its messy angst, evoked in the same breath as the Asian megacity Singapore. Singapore brings to mind an efficient nanny state, the bustling financial centre of Asia, or an air-conditioned, sanitized nation, but rarely unfettered creativity. On 16 November 2014, however, poetry advocates in Singapore managed to brilliantly showcase the pulsing heart of the people most invisible in Singaporean society: the foreign migrant worker.

The first-ever Migrant Workers Poetry Competition, organized by Banglar Kantha and Dibashram, was held at the National Library of Singapore. In the spirit of Transient Workers Count Too (TWC2), about a hundred guests crammed into the lecture hall-style classroom on the fifth floor of the National Library to listen to the poetic words of migrant workers whose day jobs involve long hours at construction sites. As migrant-worker advocate Debbie Fordyce said in her introductory speech, Singaporeans often do not see these workers beyond their tasks.

Yet here they were, confidently reading poems in their mother tongues. Students from the United World College helped recite the English translations for an enraptured audience, who were quickly caught up in the web of words spun by Monir Ahmod, who was the first to perform. Ahmod, who writes under the pseudonym Shromik (Worker) and is a rebel poet, writes in *Pother Shishu* (*Street Child*):

> *You look for new flavours*
> *You celebrate Eid*
> *and forget to look*
> *at the hunger*
> *of the child on the street.*

Thirty-six-year-old construction supervisor and freelance journalist Zakir Hussain Khokhon from Bangladesh won first prize with his poem 'Pocket 2', which beat eighty other submissions. His poem is filled with nostalgia for the homeland and lover he has left behind:

> *Still in the same world, we belong to different spheres*
> *You on that side and me on this:*
> *we can do nothing but remember each other*
> *the memories of you and me hang like posters . . .*

He ends with the lines '*Do I really write poems / Or do my poems cry with me?*' This poem, inspired by a goodbye scene with his wife when he left for Singapore, speaks volumes about the loneliness of these men, who are able to see their loved ones once a year only if they are lucky; most wait years to go home, preferring to save their money instead.

Naturally, love appears as a theme in many poems, as do visions of loved ones left behind. There is also a strong sense of anomie in the work of many poets, as well as the sense of being a cog in the global economy. N. Regarajan, whose *Soozhnilai Sollidhandavai* (Tamil) won third place, writes: '*Money / A peculiar disease . . . / Money alone / kills by absence*'.

Organizer Shivaji Das, a volunteer with TWC2, is already busy organizing more poetry competitions featuring migrant workers. The next one is being planned in neighbouring Malaysia, and another one later, in South Korea. There are also plans of eventually publishing an anthology of poems from such contests.

Das describes receiving handwritten entries, some scribbled on any loose paper available to the workers, as these men have no leisure time to write and often compose poems while travelling to their worksite and back on company-provided transport. They are free only on Sunday evenings, which they use to socialize; some have access to email and Facebook, but others don't have spare money for mobile phone credits.

The first-place winner of the poetry competition received a cash prize of S$200 ($160), the runner-up S$100, while third place was awarded S$50. The poems were written in Bengali and Tamil and other languages of the Indian subcontinent. Jibon, who placed second in the competition, was born in Bangladesh and works in a shipyard; Rengarajan, from India, works in construction. The volunteer translators involved in the project included Gopika Jadeja, Debabrata Basu, Shivaji Das, and Souradip Bhattacharya, Krishna Udayshankar, Shobhana Udayshankar, and Vinod Krishnan.

According to Alvin Pang, a leading Singaporean poet who was a judge and sponsor for the event, it took just one and a half months from the inception to hold the competition. He would also like to see the migrant worker poetry project featured in Singapore's annual literary festival: 'I truly do believe that the Singapore Writers Festival would benefit from such engagement. So much talent, so much to share and learn!'

The British poet George Szirtes blogged about the event:

> The construction workers—since that is what they mostly are—
> are confident in delivery, some dramatic, some song-like, some

gesticulating, some very still. Some of them have published back home. Some are primarily political. There is a poem celebrating May Day that distances itself from both the political left and the right. . . . Here they are, for the very first time in public, recognized for the creative human personalities they are, not just lost figures in the distance.

This would be a wonderful initiative in any country, but especially timely in Singapore, as riots had erupted on the streets of Little India in December 2013, sparked by the death of a thirty-three-year-old man knocked down by a private bus. About four hundred foreign workers had then taken to the streets, hurling railings at police and torching police cars and an ambulance. Such street violence in a country so controlled had met with a strong backlash, both by the Singaporean authorities and Singaporean citizens. In multicultural and multilingual Singapore, where street signs frequently appear in four languages (English, Mandarin Chinese, Malay, and even Tamil), the migrant populations and their space in a larger Singaporean identity have long been a cause for contentious scrutiny.

Hena Roy, a Singaporean who was a part of the audience, wrote on Facebook:

So much of pain in their poems! Some workers with diplomas are here digging and drilling under all weathers and treated like 'animals' sometimes. I hear the expletives spewed in Hokkien at this group of people, especially when they are new to Singapore. Many a time I walked away (no more henceforth) because I couldn't take it.

But on the night of the competition, the poets took centre stage, closing the door on the drudgery of their daily lives. While the judges deliberated over the winners, there was music and dance and the audience clapped and danced along, everyone united in the same music and rhythm. There were drums, guitar, and a harmonium, merging with the voices of the singers. One of the poets had written the words to one of the songs, and he was the first to dance. The mood was festive, unfettered.

Judge Kirpal Singh, a Singaporean poet and academic, delighted the contestants by referring to the works of Rabindranath Tagore, the first non-European to win the Nobel Prize in Literature in 1913; Tagore's work, too, was written in Bengali.

Migrant workers in too many parts of the world lead hard lives and are frequently treated as both faceless and voiceless automatons. In September 2014 the world was shocked by the story of a twenty-four-year-old migrant worker in the southern Chinese city of Shenzhen, Xu Lizhi, who jumped out of the window of a residential dormitory and committed suicide.

A poetry competition like this is a wonderful beginning, a laudable chance to hear the voices from the liminal edges of the many societies we live in. Instead of looking away, we need to hear what these poets have to say about our common humanity. Rajeeb Shil Jibon, who won second prize, writes in *Aadho aalo aadho andhar* (*Shades of light and dark*):

> *Perhaps I am waiting for a time*
> *An impression, a smell or an empty house*
> *A feeling of silent tiredness*
> *Walking down the path of prose that excites my soul.*

Misogyny in Bengali Nursery Rhymes

I recently had the opportunity to moderate the Q&A session after a viewing of *Shonar Pahar, The Golden Mountain,* at the 2018 Chicago South Asian Film Festival. This gave me the opportunity to think about Bengali cinema—and Bengali poetry—in a way I haven't consciously processed in many years.

Shonar Pahar pays tribute to a childlike wonder about the world and the director, Parambrata Chattopadhyay, beautifully weaves a story about the power of the imagination to create an alternative joyful universe even when the reality is rather bleak. This is a nuanced, gentle, story of the magical friendship between a seventy-year-old woman and a seven-year-old boy. However, the use of a Tagore poem, *Birpurush*, as a trope in this movie was problematic.

This much-venerated poem has become a classic of Bengali literature and the patriarchy inherent in the fable of a little boy, single-handedly saving his mother from dacoits in the deep dark jungle, was very much a product of the time it was written.

Iconic or not, how likely would it be that a feisty single mother—and a librarian with a wealth of literary texts at her disposal—would so worship a poem about little boys being their mothers' saviours? The intertextuality with *Birpurush* made me question the director on whether the movie could have been more nuanced when it came to gender roles in this movie, or whether that would be unrealistic.

As I thought about the treatment of this single poem in this movie, I also thought hard about the Bengali poems from my own childhood, which made me, as a young girl, feel brave or empowered.

I could not think of a single one.

The Bengalis have a wonderful tradition of intelligent nonsense rhymes and playful neologisms like *HaJaBaRaLa* and *Abol Tabol* but it requires some intellectual maturity to figure out the irony behind the characterization of the 'perfect' groom Gangaram (*Sat Patro*). By that time, girls have been already been indoctrinated into Bengali folk tales—*Rup Katha*—populated by a harem of jealous queens who bury seven brothers and their single sister alive until they bloom into champa flowers (*Shaat Bhai Champa*); jealous sisters who give away the Queen's three children (*Arun, Barun, Kiranmala*); a jealous queen who wants to bathe in her two stepsons' blood (*Basanta ar Hemanta*). Grown women are evil connivers who wield power disgracefully; little girls have no agency except that of mild goodness. and are invariably outnumbered by male siblings.

From babyhood, girls are lulled to sleep with poems about swinging in the air, comb in hair, waiting for a groom to sweep them off:

দোল দোল দুলুনি
রাঙা মাথায় চিরুনি
বর আসবে এখুনি
নিয়ে যাবে তখুনি

Swing, swing, on the swing,
Red comb through your hair,
A groom is now arriving,
To take you away from here

Another about a new bride, speechless with shyness:

আতা গাছে তোতা পাখি
ডালিম গাছে মৌ,
এত ডাকি তবু কথা
কও না কেন বৌ?

On the custard-apple tree, a parrot,
on the pomegranate bush, a bee,
Bride, I've tried so hard to make you speak
Won't you speak to me?

The most memorable nursery rhyme is about a young girl's wedding:

চাঁদ উঠেছে, ফুল ফুটেছে,
কদম তলায় কে?
হাতি নাচছে, ঘোড়া নাচছে,
সোনামণির বে।

The moon is up, the flowers bloom
Who sits under the kadam tree?
Elephants dance, horses sway,
It's my darling's wedding day.

But the wedding arena is not exclusive to girls, shared as it is with a bat wedding (*Adur badur chalta badur*), and little boys marching to their brides accompanied by 600 drummers (*Dol dol dol . . . khokha jabe biye korte shaate chhosho dhol*), then another goes to his wedding accompanied by a tomcat (*Ghore ache hulo beral komor bedheche*).

Rhymes abound with little boys dancing and animals being exhorted to watch (*Ai re ai tiye . . . ore bhodor phire cha, Khokar nachon dekhe ja*); elder brothers randomly cruel to fish (*Noton noton payra guli . . . dadar haate kolom chilo churey mereche*); boys watching the dangerous play of frogs on the heads of snakes (*Shaaper mathai baeng nachuni, cheye dekho na khoka moni*). In these poems, little girls are absent.

The moon is a maternal uncle (*Aye aye Chandmama . . .*), but the dispenser of sleep is an aunt, called in to—you guessed it—spread sleep on infant male eyes (*Ghumparani mashi pishi . . . Khokar chokhe ghum nai, ghum diye jeyo*).

It may seem silly to complain about misrepresentation from a different time (who thinks of Catholic priests and sex when reciting *Goosey Goosey Gander* any more?) but representation matters. If we are still teaching little girls from babyhood that they are invisible or less worthy of being seen, it has real repercussions. The language used to frame the girls born into our homes triumphs over any tradition of chanting mantras at our clay goddesses.

India as a whole has a problem with child marriage; Bengal ranks fourth in child marriages nationwide. A 2008 survey found that 54.7 per cent of currently married women aged 20–24 in Bengal were married before the age of eighteen as a child bride.[6] Still, nobody thinks about child brides while sing-songing about little girls getting married under the full moon with adorably footloose elephants and horses. Bangla nursery compilations are now on YouTube, animated with Pixar-inspired goggle-eyed children, but the lyrics remain largely true to the originals.

When I asked the director—and lead actor—of *Shonar Pahar*, whether the poem *Birpurush* was an appropriate refrain for this particular movie, he replied that he had based the

---

6 Ghosh, Biswajit. (2011). 'Child Marriage, Society and the Law: A Study in a Rural Context in West Bengal, India'. *International Journal of Law Policy and the Family*. 25. 199–219. 10.1093/lawfam/ebr002.

character on his own mother, and made the movie as a homage to their own interactions, not questioning the choice of the poem deeply. However, as creative artists, we all tread a fine line between verisimilitude and genuflecting on the archaic, surely? Asking uncomfortable questions is only the beginning.

A Shradhanjali for Derek Walcott, from Chicago

In Indian culture, after the passing of a revered and beloved person, we offer a Shradhanjali, a tribute filled with veneration. This is mine, for Sir Derek Walcott. I consider myself an Indian-American-Malaysian writer-poet and Sir Walcott's poetry has touched me in different countries, in several key phases of my own creative life.

On 6 June 2013, the Poetry Foundation in Chicago hosted the Chicago segment of the Poetry Society of America's 2013 national series, *Yet Do I Marvel: Black Iconic Poets of the Twentieth Century*. I chose to speak about Derek Walcott, and this essay is from my notes from that evening.

Chicago is as much home to me as is Kuala Lumpur and New Delhi, so I chose Walcott, another nomad poet, who writes about exile and politics and post-colonial identity in a voice resonant with many languages. He claims the brilliance of a tropical monsoon sky while in the bone-chilling winds of an American winter. Although Walcott is of a generation earlier than mine his concerns will unfortunately remain relevant to the generation that comes after me. The world still remains divided by wars, endangered by racial violence and religious distrust ... and still, largely driven by greed.

Walcott's international sensibility speaks of the Caribbean, Africa, Europe and America with the same familiarity, and he negotiates the difficult, often dangerously fraught, spaces in between.

So, I will begin with the problems with writing in language gifted by colonial masters in his poem 'A Far Cry From Africa':

> *Again brutish necessity wipes its hands*
> *Upon the napkin of a dirty cause, again*
> *A waste of our compassion, as with Spain,*
> *The gorilla wrestles with the superman.*
> *I who am poisoned with the blood of both,*
> *Where shall I turn, divided to the vein?*
> *I who have cursed*
> *The drunken officer of British rule, how choose*
> *Between this Africa and the English tongue I love?*
> *Betray them both, or give back what they give?*
> *How can I face such slaughter and be cool?*
> *How can I turn from Africa and live?*

Even in a poem describing the slaughter of Africa, Walcott sings with rhyme and metre.

As a child, I was brought up on Bengali poetry written by another Nobel Laureate, Rabindranath Tagore, whose poems are literally sung in the homes of West Bengal and of Bangladesh; even the Bengali diaspora sings this poetry. I grew up with an appreciation of the musicality of poetry, but through the musicality of his writing, Walcott showed me how to use words to be the change in this world. My own recent writing, about the deep racial divides in Malaysia, or about the victims of the Wisconsin Sikh temple shooting made invisible in the American media, or about the New Delhi rapes—all these poems believe, perhaps a little naively, that poetry can be powerful harbingers of change. At a literary festival in Thailand, I heard Kim Jong

Il's former court-poet read a poem about a woman selling her daughter in a marketplace (the child is bought by a soldier), and it moved the jaded international audience in a way news reports rarely do. At a literary festival in Myanmar, fiery monks in red robes quizzed poets about the value of poetry in challenging notions of nationalism.

Poets such as Derek Walcott have illuminated our way of writing poetry about the dispossessed.

It is impossible to talk of Walcott without referring to the Homeric epic poem, 'Omeros'. I was working on a sociolinguistics project for six years in Leiden, the Netherlands; Leiden is an ancient cobblestoned city of poetry, the birthplace of Rembrandt. The walls of this city has poems in different languages inscribed on street corners, and on the walls of the KITLV library, which houses a fantastic Caribbean and Southeast Asian collection, I would come face to face with these lines from 'Omeros' every single day:

> *This was the shout on which each odyssey pivots,*
> *that silent cry for a reef, or familiar bird,*
> *not the outcry of battle, not the tangled plots*
> *of a fishnet, but when a wave rhymes with one's grave,*
> *a canoe with a coffin, once that parallel*
> *is crossed, and cancels the line of master and slave.*
> *Then an uplifted oar is stronger than marble*
> *Caesar's arresting palm, and a swift outrigger*
> *fleeter than his galleys in its skittering bliss.*

So much said in such brevity . . . the heart of an exile, the enchantment of a journey, the simple joys of land and sea over the trappings of entrenched power. My first poetry book is titled *The Palimpsest of Exile.*

In my own nomadic journey, I have found Chicago in Walcott's *Midsummer Poems*, in the lines:

> *Chicago's avenues, as white as Poland.*
> *A blizzard of heavenly coke hushes the ghettos.*
> *The scratched sky flickers like a TV set.*

I have found the intense heat followed by the monsoon of a New Delhi summer in these words from *The Prodigal*:

> *The dialect of the scrub in the dry season*
> *withers the flow of English. Things burn for days . . .*
> *Every noun is a stump with its roots showing,*
> *and the creole language rushes like weeds*
> *until the entire island is overrun,*
> *then the rain begins to come in paragraphs*
> *and hazes this page, hazes the grey of islets,*
> *the grey of eyes, the rainstorm's wild-haired beauty.*

Now that this voice is silent, I think of *White Egrets*, a remarkable book written by Walcott at the age of eighty. He wonders whether these poems might be his last, and says:

> *be grateful that you wrote well in this place,*
> *let the torn poems sail from you like a flock*
> *of white egrets in a long last sigh of relief.*

The last poem in *White Egrets* is 'Untitled' as Death tends to be, reducing us all to a memory to be slowly erased from the world'. But even in this, Walcott's words sing of the resurgent creative power of the word, the sheer magic of creating a vision on white paper with only black lines and creating a 'self-naming' universe as real as the one we live in:

> *This page is a cloud between whose fraying edges*
> *a headland with mountains appears brokenly*
> *then is hidden again until what emerges*
> *from the now cloudless blue is the grooved sea*
> *and the whole self-naming island, its ochre verges,*
> *. . . into the widening harbour of a town with no noise,*
> *its streets growing closer like a print you can now read,*
> *two cruise ships, schooners, a tug, ancestral canoes,*
> *as a cloud slowly covers the page and it goes*
> *white again and the book comes to a close.*

Thank you, Sir Derek Walcott. A difficult man, a problematic mentor, certainly when it came to women. This shradhanjali is to the art, a tribute to the immortality of the word, of his poetry, not to the flawed man. A deeply flawed legacy, but his words have enriched my life.

Through the Lens of Danish Siddiqui

On the morning of Friday 23 July 2021, I woke up to the news that award-winning Reuters photojournalist Danish Siddiqui was no more; he had been killed while covering clashes between Afghanistan security forces and the Taliban in Kandahar city. The last image on his Twitter feed is of security forces silhouetted against the darkening sky, the barrel of a gun clearly visible.

This picture took me back to another image, where the human face is also in silhouette. Siddiqui's picture of a three-year-old homeless boy, Sarwar, sleeping in a hammock along a sidewalk in Mumbai was taken on 7 March 2012. In it we see an embryonic being, the colour and texture of the cloth a vision of a womb-like sac, suspended in our mind's eye in a place before birth. This picture could have easily taken on the tropes of poverty-porn and shown Sarwar with a runny nose clinging to a bite of foraged food, especially as the photojournalism from the streets of India have made such images into viable pieces of commerce. Instead, Siddiqui takes Sarwar's image and gives him the humanity of being—at three years—still a baby, any baby, *our* baby. The viewer is transfixed by the exquisite wonder in this image, the darker foetal shadow of the boy, like a sonograph, juxtaposed under his features in repose.

Siddiqui brought his empathetic gaze to many images like this, as he continued to photograph national and global emergencies. As the chief of Reuters Pictures multimedia team in India, in the last years he captured key moments of the unfolding COVID crisis in India, the protests against the Citizenship Amendment Act in 2020, the North East Delhi riots, and the migrant workers' exodus during India's first lockdown. He also covered the Rohingya genocide in Myanmar and asylum seekers in Switzerland, the 2015 Nepal earthquake, pro-democracy protests in Hong Kong, and the Easter bomb blasts in Sri Lanka in 2019, among other global events.

A picture of a Rohingya refugee after crossing the Bay of Bengal was taken when Siddiqui and his colleagues were part of the Reuters team that won the 2018 Pulitzer Prize. The woman's face is obscured, and her body has fallen on the sand either in gratitude or exhaustion ... or both. There is the hull of a small wooden boat in the distance, still disgorging men from its tight confines. Smoke billows at a distance. There is so much in this frame to process, but instead of our voyeuristic pity, it is the possibility of hope that is foregrounded.

In an interview with *Scroll.in* in 2018, Siddiqui said an image 'should draw people and tell them the whole story without being loud'. His quietude is especially powerful in the pictures taken after the bomb blasts in Sri Lanka on Easter Sunday in 2019, one of a series of coordinated attacks by suicide bombers that killed more than 250 people. He photographed empty houses: red curtains surrounding a rumpled bed; a lone schoolchild's backpack, the blue mosquito net falling like a shroud; a bright green autorickshaw tethered among verdant foliage, the driver no longer alive.

In an India that is becoming intolerant of any dissent, Siddiqui's powerful lenses earned the wrath of the government, and the Hindutva trolls on social media. With the famous photo of a mob beating up a lone man, Siddiqui shone the spotlight on the rabid mob, not on the victim, and demonstrated the implications of silence. A group of men shouting pro-Hindu slogans beating a Muslim man during protests sparked by the Citizenship Amendment Act in Delhi on 24 February 2020 highlighted a national complicity in the erosion of the secularism that India had always stood for.

And that resplendent image of the flag fluttering over the heads of thousands of protesting farmers? What is visible in Siddiqui's stunning iconography is that at stake, is the soul of India, through the livelihood of those that feed the nation. It is a poster for a movement still unresolved.

His uncompromising images of the burning pyres at the height of the COVID crisis sparked outrage at a time when the Indian government was trying to minimize the problem. Yet, even here, where death visited so many families, Siddiqui drew his lenses away from tear-streaked faces and looked instead at a huddle of mourners, a man in full PPE gear barely standing in a barren field, the sardine-can crowding of heads and feet in a hospital.

In an age of reality TV where journalists and viewers alike blur the lines between consent and voyeurism, stripping the human subject of any dignity in moments of abject grief, Siddique was, first and foremost, a chronicler of absence. Absence of distinctive facial features, of signages, of place names. He rendered the particular universal by the lack of labels, and in doing so, he dragged us all into stories of our shared humanity. He refused to let us pity the victim before quickly turning away, relieved to be unscathed. In the probe of his lens, we are all complicit.

On Siddiqui's profile page on the Reuters website, the last line reads, 'I respect my subjects the most—they give me my inspiration.' That is clear from his work, and as journalism attempts at a certain objectivity, Danish Siddiqui succeeded in that too many of us will recognize his iconic pictures without knowing anything about the man behind the lens. Although some of his best work came from conflict zones, he also chronicled the minutiae of everyday life: a blind singer on a train, a child on the shoulders of his migrant-worker father headed back to their village in a lockdown; a soldier in full fatigues eating ice cream. He filed stories every week, and his egalitarian lens showed up in places where we could not— would not—venture. The absence of such a talent is a grievous loss for the world.

The Advantage of the (Global)
Asian Writer

Asian writers, as well as writers of Asian descent, face unique publishing challenges in Western markets. They are frequently expected to conform to stereotypical tales of terrorism and gender discrimination written into family sagas, if not outright poverty porn. Writers have been striking back with stories that attempt to rephrase the narrative into a less exotic post-colonial idea of Asia, but as the annual VIDA: Women in Literary Arts count and other surveys demonstrate, the publishing world is still unfairly skewed along race and gendered lines.

Online databases for international journals and prizes have somewhat destabilized the old power structures, but despite the democratization of the internet through submission portals like Submittable and other platforms, the lack of mentors and MFA programmes in Asia often hobbles the emerging writer, especially as a steady internet connection, or even access to computers, is still is a luxury for many writers living in the smaller Asian cities. Countries in Southeast Asia—like Malaysia and Singapore—have started to offer home-grown writing contests and are regularly publishing writers in paid anthologies, making the field more level for those who write for Asian audiences rooted in Asian sensibilities.

As I currently teach writing courses in many parts of the world, I often consider the ways that Asian writers can tap into the existing markets available worldwide, and stand out by the kind of writing they offer, and even some of the unseen advantages of global Asian writing.

* * *

Asia is not a monolithic idea, with forty-eight countries in Asia and three Oceanic sub-regions, and writers from these various cultures, states and cities, and starting to make a multitudinous variety of voices heard, adding much needed diversity and representation to the English cannon. The experience of Dhan Gopal Mukerji, who won the Newbery Medal in 1928 and carved out a writing career in the US at a time of blatant racism in immigration policies shows that the challenges and opportunities have always been there, but with caveats. Modern Asian writers are less willing to accept token representation and are making their numbers felt and voices heard through a body of pioneering works published online and in print. They are winning contests and prizes. The big questions motivating this personal essay are: Are the big contests and prizes even available to the Asian writer? In the absence of established MFA programmes and large writing residencies in Asian cities, can winning a prize make a difference in the Asian writer's career trajectory?

By the time I reached Bali on 22 October 2017, I had already been out of my home in Chicago for over two months. I was mentally and physically drained by a book tour but due to deliver a keynote at the Asia Pacific Writers and Translators Annual Conference in two days. My talk, being publicized as 'Contests and Prizes: The Advantage of the (Global) Asian Writer', was becoming impossible to write.

Two novels, yet I still felt the imposter syndrome growing toxic in my brain. What could I possibly say to a group of

Asian and Pacific writers gathered in Bali, especially to those with hyphenated identities like mine, the Indian-American, the Australian-Malaysian . . . this was a gathering of the many literary talents of our global world, all containing multitudes.

I can only tell my own story. In this global age, our stories resonate with many, and mine, of a lifetime lived on different continents, is perhaps not so different after all. This was my third Asia Pacific Writers and Translators (APWT) conference; what I especially loved about APWT is that there is a genuine effort to be a Pan-Asia Pacific group that welcomes both writers and translators. A good number of APWT writers have become good friends and this is a collegial, cosy group, with none of the literary casteism that festivals with more star power inevitably attract.

The only reason I had been asked to deliver this lecture at all is that I had two novels published in 2016. *Ode to Broken Things* had been longlisted for the Man Asian Literary Prize as an unpublished novel in 2009, and *Shambala Junction* had just won the Virginia Prize for Fiction. Both novels were published in the UK (although *Ode to Broken Things* had been previously published as *Thunder Demons* in 2011 for the South Asian market).

As an Asian writer who writes about Asia—Malaysia and India in particular—my path to publication, and winning prizes, has been both rocky and unpredictable. As a child of a diplomat, wanderlust kissed my feet at a very young age, and as an adult, I have lived and worked in many cities, not in a sabbatical year or any sort of short layover, but committing my life to a new place for three years or more at a time.

I know well that our Asian stories are still largely untold, and sometimes deliberately unheard, in English-language publishing. Sometimes, I was able to leverage that difference (Political Fiction on Malaysia? What?) and everyone from

Arundhati Roy's agent to Jhumpa Lahiri's agent asked immediately to read the complete manuscript. But it wasn't until my debut novel was longlisted for the Man Asian Literary Prize in 2009, that I was faced with a flurry of interest from literary agents, after which one signed me on to the road to publication. Being longlisted for a major prize—despite the fact that I had actually won nothing—gave a wonderful fillip to my career and stopped agents from returning the manuscript with read-between-the-lines disinterest like: 'Your novel is too political for America.'

I strongly advise anyone who is still looking for recognition and some validation to start submitting your work immediately for publication. Submit promiscuously and often. There are a lot of online journals and magazines devoted to Asian writing, and looking for new and established writers. *Jaggery*, where I am a contributing editor, is a paying market. It is imperative to get some publications under your belt, preferably by collecting some bylines where editors are willing to part with money to showcase your work.

Then submit your work for some major awards and prizes.

Don't listen to the roadblockers and naysayers. The only reason I submitted my debut novel to the Man Asian Literary Prize in the first place was because a half-hearted agent had told me that my work was very readable, but unlikely to win any prizes. I had a poetry chapbook accepted by a Canadian press that year and already had a number of short stories placed in journals, and I was determined to prove her wrong. Submit because you have faith in your work and are determined to be a published author someday, and just keep submitting. No one else can do that necessary work for you.

There are some globally competitive prizes which will bring you to the attention of a world stage: The Commonwealth Short Story Prize, The Sunday Times EFG Short Story

Award, Bridport. Look for contests that will cost you little or nothing to submit. The APWT page has a listing of Call for Submissions specifically addressed to Asia-Pacific writers, but also keeps tracking local contests. I have bookmarked sites like Poets and Writers (P&W); P&W offers a searchable database, but is most overwhelmingly skewed towards writers in the US.

Asia's population is equivalent to 60 per cent of the total world population, and when we speak of Asian literature, it seems precocious to even describe it as if it were one homogenous tradition. A veteran of literary festivals in Myanmar and China and Malaysia and Singapore, I am still astonished at the variety of stories and fables I have yet to discover.

In Asia, we live in exciting and turbulent times, with the kind of political and social upheavals that mined gold for South American writing, when fiction and factions turned into astonishing magical realism. Neighbouring countries in Europe—Germany, the Netherlands, Brussels—seem unvaried when we consider the diversity in of Asian neighbours like Malaysia, Thailand and Laos, with completely different cultural artefacts, food, and even languages. We have oceans of stories to tell and have barely wet our toes.

Markets, as you will find, are also very different. The appetite for ghosts and pontianaks and flesh-eating deviants seems unflagging in Southeast Asia, the stuff of some of the basest melodramas. Yet an old fable in a new context, in the hands of a master storyteller, Alyssa Wong's *Hungry Daughters of Starving Mothers* deservedly won the Nebula Award in 2015. Usman T. Malik, a Pakistani writer who publishes prolifically in the US, is a master of short fiction and rewrites the rules of writing horror with a dash of myth and magic. Shiv Ramdas's short story *And Now His Lordship Is Laughing* is set during the Bengal famine of 1943 and was nominated for both the 2020 Hugo Award for Best Short Story and the 2020 Nebula Award for Best Short Story; He describes himself as a writer of post-colonial speculative fiction—from science fiction and fantasy to horror and everything in between.

Genres are porous and the world is thirsty for our stories.

In poetry, Asian-American writers like Ocean Vuong (2018 T.S. Eliot Prize) and Vijay Sheshadri (2014 Pulitzer) have been winning prizes for writing with a very strong Asian sensibility. Tishani Doshi is rewriting fables in verse for the twenty-first century and the 2015 T.S. Eliot prize winner, Sarah Howe, starts with an old Chinese proverb, then takes on commerce and patriarchy and female resilience in a way that is breathtakingly universal:

TAME

It is more profitable to raise geese than daughters.
                  —CHINESE PROVERB

> *This is the tale of the woodsman's daughter.*
> *Born with a box*
>   *of ashes set beside the bed,*
> *in case. Before the baby's first cry, he rolled her*
> *face into the cinders—*
>   *held it. Weak from the bloom*
> *of too-much-blood, the new mother tried to stop*
> *his hand. He dragged*
>   *her out into the yard, flogged her . . .*

It still feels harder for an Asian writer to break through into the mainstream English-language publishing world, and it is, with too many publishers opting for a token representation instead of aiming for a true variety of voices. When I first started publishing, there was a strong demand for immigrant stories where publishers could slap on the cover a bare-shouldered sari-draped silhouette; such stereotypes are thankfully getting harder to spot on airport shelves now.

It is also important to remember that Asian writers have always battled odds to be read by English-speaking audiences, and still triumphed. While at the historic Strand Bookstore in New York recently, I found next to my books, a Dhan Gopal Mukerji.

This Mukerji—no relation—had won the Newbery Medal in 1928 and had carved out a writing career in the US at a time of blatant racism in immigration policies. He was the first successful Indian writer there to be published by the large publishing houses, and he pre-dates G.V. Desani and Mulk Raj Anand by a decade and more. However, despite his fame and success, he felt deeply isolated and marginalized in the US and committed suicide in 1936 in Connecticut, after which, his work largely faded into obscurity.

In 1913, Rabindranath Tagore, won the Nobel Prize for *Song Offerings* (*Geetanjali*), while living and working in India. Yet when Bob Dylan won the 2016 Nobel Prize for essentially writing song lyrics, this attracted the ire of writers of the world. Few know, or remember, that Tagore was the first writer to win the Nobel for poetic lyrics—literally his offering of songs—103 years earlier. Tagore may still loom large over the Bengali imagination, but outside Bengal, he is now largely forgotten, or worse, considered overrated.

Asian writers have always been corralling a readership by winning prizes, in times much worse than our own. And that the hunger for Asian writing which startles in different ways, will always be there, as the Swedish Academy member, Horace Engdahl, said in his controversial statement in 2014. On 'our western side that there is a problem, because when reading many writers from Asia and Africa, one finds a certain liberty again.'

Andrew Kidd, in establishing the Folio Prize said, '. . . certainly the case that some of the strongest new voices in literature are emerging from those places where change is dramatic rather than incremental, from where the news is most urgent to report, and the global outlook of the Folio prize was designed to capture these voices . . .'

The good news is that with Asian wealth growing, multinational publishers are swarming the Indian and Chinese publishing markets. Penguin Random House is operating from Singapore, and has offices in India and China. When I started to publish in 2002, from Singapore, I was able to walk into the offices of Penguin Books in New Delhi with just my business card. Even today, many of the large Indian publishing houses read unsolicited and un-agented submissions. Although having an agent substantially improves the chances of getting published, it is still not a precondition for Asia, as it is in the US. In Malaysia and Singapore, the growth of publishing houses like Epigram, Fixi and Maya means that in a number of ways, the doors seem more open in Asia, for local writing.

As a side effect, publishing in Asian journals and anthologies is also getting more lucrative in the face of growing competition. *The Mekong Review* continues to startle and delight with its range of reporting and stories from Asia.

Of course, the Asian diaspora and Asians within Asia face very different challenges. Asian writers living in Asia often feel they are on their own; well, because they actually are. Although I am not a fan of the MFA model, the American MFA allows a degree of networking and access to publishing professionals that writers in Asian cities can only dream about. Some MFAs are fully funded, and regional and national foundations also offer money to writers. In comparison, state-sponsored aid in Asia, whether in India or Malaysia, is so structured on language chauvinism that it may as well not exist for a large segment of the population.

When I taught Creative Writing at the Indian Institute of Technology in New Delhi, there was such a paucity of writing courses in India that students brought their friends to audit classes. I have taught Junot Diaz's profanity-laced dialogues and Maya Angelou's southern speech (and had to explain the rules of codeswitching and Black English Vernacular) to students in dhotis who were taking my class in a monastic order in West Bengal. In challenges, there are deeply rewarding opportunities.

So to all of you out there, established writers or struggling, I'd urge you to pay forward the help you have received along the way. There are so many ways to promote other Asian voices and practise good literary citizenship:

Promote Asian Writers

Try to promote Asian writing on Goodreads, Amazon, blogs and social media, whenever possible. There is some fantastic writing by women from Asia or of Asian descent and although I am often left cold by American fiction that burns up the bestseller lists with multi-starred reviews (the stories of immigration and assimilation seem especially tired), when a story like *Ghachar Ghochar*—by Vivek Shanbhag, translated by Srinath Perur from Kannada—hits the bestseller list, it is very sweet indeed. Sarah Thankam Matthews projects the gritty reality of belonging in multiple places and feeling at home in none in her debut novel *All This Could Be Different*. Told in pitch-perfect prose, this is a novel that defies the myth of the model immigrant (this book was a finalist for the 2022 National Book Award for Fiction).

I have also been a part of writing and critique groups in Chicago, Shanghai, Amsterdam, Singapore and Kuala

Lumpur . . . State censorship is not a reason to stop writing. Create a network of writers who understand words and concepts without glossaries so that the writing remains strong and undiluted.

Include Asian Writers in your Teaching Curriculum

If you are a teacher or instructor or professor, think of ways to include Asian writers in your curriculum. I was thrilled to find that a teacher had recently initiated a World Cup for Literature structured along the lines of the more famous Soccer World Cup. By using short stories available online (this class used the *World Literature Today* archives), they avoided the costs of expensive textbooks, and kept the stories current and topical. This is a brilliant idea to encourage close reading and creative thinking among students, while pitting stories against each other in a playful but exciting 'national award'.

Start an Asian Writing Award

When my father-in-law passed away in 2015, I wanted to commemorate his memory in a way that transcended the misogynistic ritualism in Hinduism. This led to the D.K. Dutt Award for Literary excellence, and I was lucky to have the exceptional editing skills of Sharon Bakar in Malaysia. Sharon also brought her expertise and network as a publisher (WordWorks) to the table when she agreed to be judge and co-editor. The first award, on the theme of sports writing, was won by Hanna Alkaf. Hanna went on to sign a contract for representation with a New York literary agency, and then a publishing contract with Simon and Schuster's *Salaam Reads*; her first YA novel was released worldwide in 2019, and she has written many more books.

The D.K. Dutt Award had a small, budgeted beginning; a literary award that promised the winners and two or three runners-up money, and everyone else a shot at publication in the anthology with a nominal payment. Writers who submitted stories for this award did not all achieve international validation, although a lot of them did go on to win other awards and recognition; Notable is Saras Manickam, who won the D.K. Dutt Award and then won the Commonwealth Short Story Prize for Asia. However, in Malaysia, as in many countries in Asia, just having another avenue to see creative work professionally edited and presented often seems like a win.

Just as the multiplicity of our cuisines is taking over cities from London to Chicago to Sydney, it would be lovely to see Asian writers mainstreamed in a similar way. Just don't hold back on the spice and flavours; give us the authentic and the heartfelt and the ancient, framed by clear new ways of seeing.

Learning Grace

A distinctive orange-yellow flower blooms my guesthouse window at Belur Math in West Bengal; it is the nagalinga. The odour is so unpleasant that the flowers work as an insect repellent when rubbed on skin or clothes.

I know the nagalinga as the 'cannonball' from Malaysia, yet the Indian version is different enough in colour and size to make me search for the similarities in the towering filigree-leaf branches. One day, the security guard reaches up and plucks a flower for me.

'Open the hood, Didi,' he urges, 'and you will see Shiva. It's the nagalinga.'

Under the hood is a white protrusion. The flower lies in my palm like a divine offering. Men like the security guard are considered simpletons for being so easily touched by grace, but I felt touched by his epiphany.

Shouldn't living life as one long miracle be as important as building edifices to faith?

* * *

In 2014, I was a Visiting Professor at the Ramakrishna Mission Vidyamandira, an undergraduate institution that is part of University of Calcutta. Situated within Belur Math and an hour's drive from Kolkata, Belur Math is the headquarters of the Ramkrishna Movement and therefore a place of religious pilgrimage. This sprawling edifice to faith takes up forty acres of land on the banks of the Ganges, and is a place of manicured lawns framing a meditative environment, a far cry from the heat and dust of Kolkata.

My students came to class in traditional dhotis topped with kurtas, open-toed sandals on their feet. The unsewn cloth circling their waist was partially hidden below hoodies in the chilly early winter mornings. The boys were not allowed to have mobile phones in 2014, although that rule would be relaxed when I taught again in 2016.

This is a place arrested in time in many ways, treating a guest like God—*Athithi Devo Bhava*—and more so when the guest is a teacher. At the Sarada Peeth where I lunch every day, within the home of the beloved matriarch of the movement, Ma Sarada, I am often the only woman in the dining hall. I am plied with food and dessert, entreated to have more, then even more, all served with the gentle admonition, 'You've come to your mother's home, she is feeding you, you cannot say no!' There are Bengali delicacies every day, served with fresh fish from the pond nearby, for Bengali monastic orders are pescatarian. Always, at the end of the meal, is a profusion of sweet, milky desserts, infused with nuts and cardamom and glazed with fruit.

Every morning, the boys take turns in pairs to deliver a hot breakfast to my guesthouse. In this monastic order where women were rarely seen, I am totally pampered and venerated.

* * *

My days are spent teaching and discussing Munroe, Hemingway, Millhauser and Murakami, for a workshop on 'Migration, Travel & the Modern Short Story'. Among other texts, I teach Junot Diaz's *Miss Lora*, hoping that this tale of performative masculinity and teenage lust will resonate with this sheltered group, but by the end of the class, I have to teach a session on academic vocabulary, and explain why the f-word is not acceptable in academic essays despite its liberal use in fiction.

This institution remains one of my favourite places to teach in; the boys engaging with the wider world while equipped with a depth of knowledge of Bengali religious and literary texts. When we discuss Angelou and Baldwin, we have a fascinating discussion on the rule-based grammar underpinning Black English vernacular, and how the English case system has lost all but the possessive case, whereas Bengali retained more of its Indo-European roots.

Every evening we break to meditate under the cathedral nave of the central temple, a building fused with the essence of many religious structures to celebrate the unity of humankind. Every evening the male baritones and sopranos would swell to a reverent crescendo like the Gregorian chants, their sonorous resonance beyond words in an attempt to kindle the presence of the divine within. Then, we would convene again for evening classes, perhaps even continue with profane Diaz.

On the anniversary of Ramakrishna's birthday, I woke to the cacophony of celebrations starting as dawn began to striate the morning sky. There was a beautiful Usha Kirtan sung as the Swamijis joyously danced their way around the many temples, accompanied by the music of the sarod with harmonium and tabla from the stage. For breakfast there was a sweet prasad, but sweetest of all were the birdcalls that morning, as birds flew from tree to majestic tree in this most festive of days.

On other days, there was the meditative peace of the Ganges in the twilight evenings. Zen when I least looked for it, and grace everywhere.

There was a rain-splattered pond outside the window, the pale-bricked buildings a haze in the distance, the damp smell of sprouting ground. A flowering jasmine scent would waft subtly into the room at night.

And amidst it all was the security guard, finding God in the quiddity of daily life, holding grace in the bloom of flowers.

Sudah Makan?

Nothing gets the Malaysian salivating—or frothing in rage—more quickly than discussing the relative merits of famous local eateries. Global Malaysians, like those in Chicago, pick at food memories like scabs; it is painful to remember the food of home, but an endless delight to pluck at memories filtered through the lens of nostalgia. Remembering food carts where cendol was sold for a few cents is a post-dinner sport, Malaysians take it online when the community is dispersed. A quick glance at the Global Malaysian Network (GMN) shows a recipe for roasted chicken feet with Coke(!), and pictures of a forty-year-old No-Name-Fish-Head-Curry stall in KL that is worth a visit.

What else should we expect from a country that says hello with 'sudah makan'?

Introducing a Food+Drink Writing Award—The Fay Khoo Award—in Malaysia in 2019 was a brilliant idea. The thing is, it feels natural to write from the heart about the gastronomic treasures so abundant in this country. Even Isabella Bird, the intrepid British explorer writing in 1883 about British Malaya, was in no way immune to nature's bounty in the tropics, despite her rather jaundiced colonial eye while enumerating the many character flaws of the local population. In her pages, even the ubiquitous nutmeg blooms like an epiphany:

> I saw for the first time the nutmeg growing in perfection. It
> was a great delight, as is the first sight of any tree or flower

well known from description. It is a beautiful tree, from forty to fifty feet high when full grown, with shining foliage, somewhat resembling that of the bay, and its fruit looks like a very large nectarine. One fully ripe was gathered for me. It had opened, and revealed the nutmeg with its dark brown shell showing through its crimson reticulated envelope of mace, the whole lying in a bed of pure white, a beautiful object.

—*The Golden Chersonese and the Way Thither*, 1883

Paul Theroux, writing almost a hundred years after Isabella Bird, is also prone to descriptions of his Asian travelling companions as caricatures from a colonial handbook. But when he describes a dining car during his railway journey through Malaysia, the writing is anything but two-dimensional:

For lunch I had my old favorite, mee-hoon soup with the partly poached egg whisked in among the Chinese cabbage, meat scraps, prawn slices, bean sprouts, rice noodles, and a number of other atomized ingredients that thicken it to the point where it can be eaten with chopsticks. There were no tables in the dining car, which was a noodles stall; there were sticky counters and stools, and Chinese sitting elbow to elbow, shaking soy sauce over their noodles and calling out to the waiters, little boys in red clogs, carrying beer bottles on tin trays.

—*The Great Railway Bazaar*, 1975

Food is often the only language of love in Asian families where love is not demonstrative but implied. The smell of a much-beloved childhood dish comforts the soul of an anguished child in a place medicine is unable to reach. Perhaps that is why, in Shirley Geok-Lin Lim's memoir, the heartbreak of homesickness while shopping in American supermarkets is really more about the loss of the communal kitchen:

. . . there was not a single scent of ripeness, a welcoming softness to suggest salivary delight, a tang whether sharp or sour promising kitchen smells and steaming dishes. The bananas were hard greenish yellow; onions in three-pound nylon sacks appeared scrubbed clean. If there was nourishing sweetness in all this warehouse of food, one would have to tear through unyielding metal, thick polyvinyl, pounds of cardboard . . . For the first year in the United States I was always hungry, a hunger that rebelled against American food.

—Among The White Moonfaces, 1996

Beth Yahp's recent memoir about food, family and home, which is as much about activist politics as it is about familial community, keeps returning to the bonds forged over food:

Above the table we are leaning away from each other, below it our thighs are glued. Jing's relaxed tonight, not trying to win over any flagging allegiances . . . not in political salesman mode. I gently blow my tea's bubbles away from its surface, sip at the hot sweet brew: tea dregs, stewed orange, swirled in condensed milk and a spoonful of sugar, then time to *tarik*, 'pull' it from one huge metallic mug to another, then pour it frothing into my waiting glass.

—Eat First Talk Later, 2015

I have many food stories: of a pescatarian meal under the Andalusian mountains, where the sky was a celestial lightshow; drinking homemade wine in remote Sikkim, served by a toothless grandmother with the widest grin; sharing candy with two children in Bhutan who were honouring their ancestral tsa tsas on a hillside; sharing a hotpot in Chengdu with Chinese colleagues who did not have the vocabulary to translate into English what we were eating. The act of feeding and feasting needs no language as we all celebrate one of the deepest and most essential joys of being alive.

Some of my favourite meals in Malaysia are from Pujobari in Port Dickson, where Malaysian Bengalis meet every Deepavali to celebrate Kali Puja as well as their appetites. So, in 2018, I titled my entry for the Fay Khoo Award *Paet Puja: How Malaysian-Bengalis Worship the Stomach*, and I wrote from deep within the recesses of a diasporic longing for community.

I did not expect to win the Fay Khoo Award. I was seated on the stage, waiting for the winner to be announced so that I could dash out and meet the motorcycle driver waiting to whisk me to another event. Instead, I saw the gracious Bettina Chua Abdullah walking to the microphone with an envelope, Datin Renee Khoo announcing my name, and magically, Jo Kukathas, someone I admire deeply from the theatre and Instant Cafe, breathing my words into life, while my husband beamed through it all.

It was a magical evening, filled with wonderful food writing. When Cheah Soon Seng's *The Banker's Dinner* was read out, it was as if we were all seated at that familiar late-night mamak stall.

So do it. Write what you love. There is an abundance of Malaysian stories, still untold. There is no reason to wait.

Voyage

The Voluptuousness of Memory

My face is a template on which people write ethnicity. On the small island of Itaparica in Brazil, I look local, and people only speak in Portuguese. I am used to this: in Malaysia, Tamilians scold me for being too proud to speak Tamil, and in Texas, a Mexican woman once shouted at me for not speaking Spanish. I have a face that blends into many places, and here, the Brazilians smile so readily.

I have come to a Sacatar residency to write a novel. Us artists are housed in a large beachside mansion with tall gates and resident guards but when I open the gate to go outside, the destitution of this island is evident in the half-built structures, and large families living together in small tenements. If it weren't for the Bahian statues placed on windows—a female form gazing into the distance, waiting—I would think I was in back in the crumbling parts of old Calcutta coexisting with the new. The vegetation is like the Klang Valley, lush with flowers that sprout variegated colour against green foliage. After the rains, which fall often, there is a dank lushness in the air.

This Brazilian island has an invincibility of spirit, and simmers with a multiplicity of stories and oral storytellers. The stories may be factual, fabulous, or magical, but they are all woven through the breeze and the sand of this land and have persisted through the centuries of slavery and colonialism and unbearable loss.

Thus this land is permeated with heft of saudade, a quintessential Portuguese word that is both nostalgia or profound melancholy, often with the subliminal knowledge that what is lost may never return. English translates it as 'missingness', but that does not convey the multitude of feelings . . . just as manja doesn't simply mean cute. Saudade is not Orhan Pamuk's hüzün of Istanbul, for it goes beyond a communal melancholy; it has no synonym in any of my four languages. Saudade is a state simultaneously evoking happiness for what was, and the sadness that it is now past, and Brazil commemorates a day of Saudade on 30 January.

Steeped in this sense of saudade, I find myself working on my first book of creative nonfiction instead, a manuscript that grows with a life of its own, like the unbridled foliage outside. This is a place that gives birth to heavy tomes. Itaparica's most famous writer is João Ubaldo Ribeiro, a homegrown hero who has a street named after him, as well as educational institutions; *An Invincible Memory*, published in English in 1989, is 504 pages of a family saga that spans 400 years. Brazil's history of cannibalism, murder, slavery, whaling, colonialism and much more is detailed in a lyricism that is gorgeous, but is heavy with history and magic realism, a cross between Herman Melville and Gabriel Garcia Marquez. As much as fiction can hold up a mirror to the reality of Brazil, this book opens doors to an unfamiliar world in a criollismo style, offering snapshots of deep prejudices as well as archetypes:

> They were sorcerers, that's what they were, witches of the night, wizardly as can be, people versed in the secrets of the Crystal Stone, of the power of souls and of the deities brought over from Africa under the worst conditions, people adept at using wild plants to infuse the most terrible poisonous philters and the most irresistible love potions, at sewing and binding spirits

through all kinds of sortileges, at seeing the future in all kinds of presages, at seeing the magical side of all things.

This island stills holds the ruins of an ancient church from the times Ribeiro writes about, for Our Lord of Vera Cruz was built by Jesuits in 1560. It is now cleaved through by a gameleira tree, sacred to the religion of candomblé. This tree possibly keeps the ruin erect, an ironic fusion of the Jesuit faith and the Afro-Brazilian religion that the current authorities are still trying to ban. There is the heft of history in the candomblé tradition that continues to flourish even as it is under siege, but amidst the beauty of these ruins, under the canopy of leaves that soars like a nave into the sky, there is also sadness. The susurration of the wind through the gameleira leaves, passing through the ancient cemetery bordering the ruins, drizzles bereavement.

When I have lunch with a Brazilian filmmaker—she is in her thirties, a new film of hers is releasing in a month—she asks me not to write about candomblé for the foreign market.

I put my fork down, baffled that she seems to be advocating self-censorship. Malaysia and India, two countries I know intimately, also have long traditions of spirit-worship and similar sentiments, I tell her.

'No, you don't understand. The Brazilian government, the Catholic church, they are trying to stop these candomblé and local spiritual practices, ban them completely. You may give them ammunition, by giving this international prominence.'

I tell her gently that international prominence, especially in fraught times, may be a good thing. That last year, Malaysia voted out the government that had been in power for sixty years, without bloodshed. I talk about art as resistance, especially by political cartoonists and graffiti artists and visual artists, who were charged with sedition but carried on.

The air stills. I can hear the five peacocks parading past the gazebo, it is so quiet. The filmmaker is offended. She says her mother forbade her to pursue writing, so she makes films now, which is a good thing.

I am a guest in this country, and it is so easy to get things wrong. I wonder if this artist's fear is representative of the many, and that is why there is a paucity of Brazilian novels in translation.

I start looking for Brazilian artists engaged with the political. The translator in Salvador hands me a copy of *Becoming Brazil*, featuring the works of two dozen Brazilian writers published as an edition of *Mānoa: A Pacific Journal of International Writing*.

I find Marcelo Rubens Paiva, writing about the disappearance of his father during the military rule in *I'm Still Here:*

> Memory isn't a rock with hieroglyphs etched into it . . .
> Memory is like sand dunes, grains of sand that move from one
> place to another, take on different forms, carried by the wind.
> A fact today can be reread another way tomorrow. Memory is
> alive . . . We think today with the help of a small portion
> of our past.

I find Jorge Amado, a writer who was a passionate communist and whose work openly talks about the social hierarchies in Brazil. And Raquel de Queiroz, who wrote forward-thinking, risqué books about women finding their sexuality and their voice in the 1930s. I start an email dialogue with Robson Vitorino, who writes about the class divide in São Paulo. There is also Cíntia Moscovich, who addresses the lives of Jews in Brazil, and Natalia Borges Polesso, a vocal political advocate for LGBTQ+ rights in Brazil.

Brazil fires my imagination in ways I had not anticipated. I wish there were books available in translation from this fascinating country for I am intoxicated by Brazilian voices by the time I leave. I am the madman in Salgado Maranhão's poem (translated by Alexis Levitin) *Delirica X*:

> *A madman sniffing*
> *at the moon*
> *captures instances of you.*
> . . .
> *And everywhere, forever,*
> *fire, water, time, and breath*
> *exclaim.*

Fortress, Feathers & Fabled Waters

The Neemrana Fort is a two-and-a-half-hour journey from Delhi. *You must go*, everyone urged in the middle of an enervating, sluggish monsoon, *it's only 122 kilometres away.*

As it happens in India, time and distance were mere numbers. We passed the Haldirams on the Delhi-Jaipur Highway and immediately slowed to a crawl as groups of orange-robed Kanwarias trudged along the barely-etched edges of the National Highway. The Kanwarias—faith travellers who are followers of Shiva—were on their way home after collecting holy water from the Ganges; their trudge back to their villages had to end with precision on the Amavasya, when the moon is invisible in the night sky.

Our driver would have followed the primary rule of the Indian Highways (*Might is Always Right*) and honked the pedestrians off the path, but the Kanwarias are often intoxicated, in very large numbers, and prone to violence. A week ago this highway had been cordoned off as they pelted stones at all the buses that crossed the area after one Kanwaria (who sustained minor injuries), was hit by a bus. So we followed the group at a walking pace, the driver flooring the accelerator whenever a break was visible. It didn't help that the Delhi-Jaipur highway was also flooded.

It took us four hours to finally reach Neemrana.

As we zoomed past the Rajasthan State pillars and turned into the road to Neemrana, it was like entering another world. There were narrow village roads, a climb up a small hill and there it was; Neemrana's massive fortress gates, with the many-levelled domed balconies and open rooftops, the graceful curve of the building spreading over a sprawling plateau covering twenty-five acres. Built in 1464 CE, the Neemrana Fort Palace was once inhabited by the descendants of Prithviraj Chauhan III, but a local fifteenth-century chieftain Nimola Meo, gave Neemrana its name. The fort still overlooks the sprawling valley with a rustic village and acres of open land, framed by the billion-year-old Aravalli ranges.

Tea was being served on many of the open balconies, and all at once, we were surrounded by the chirps and flaps of the feathered guests. A rose-ringed parakeet goose-stepped up to the wrought-iron chairs painted in sky blue. A purple sunbird sucked on a spiky flaming-red flower. A beautiful laughing dove gracefully skittered over the cannon before flying away. Then, as if this colourful menagerie was not welcome enough, there was the gentle rumble of thunder as an iridescent peacock unfolded his plumes in the distance, shaded by leafy bush.

The property of this stepped palace is spread over ten levels, rewarding the intrepid explorer with serendipitous views. The steps were sometimes wet and often smelt of mould (it was the monsoon after all!) Opposite Jharoka Mahal was a palace still being renovated; when we opened the door, beyond the mildew, there was a fluttering of dark wings. The picturesque names of the palaces evoke the romance of a bygone era: there is the Chandra Mahal *(Palace of the Moon)*, Sheesh Mahal *(Palace of Mirrors)*, Badal Mahal *(Palace of Clouds)* and Adi Mahal *(Primordial Palace)*, as well as the Kailash Burj *(Himalayan Turret)* and Ambar Burj *(Sky Turret)*. The whole fort seems, at

times, to be a large Hara Mahal *(Shiva's Palace)*, for Shivlings
and stone snakes, as well as other manifestations of Shiva, can
be found in many courtyards' hidden nooks and crannies.

There is a picturesque eighteenth-century stepwell nearby,
best accessed by camel-cart. Our camel, Sikandar, looked as
imperious as his name, but our first impressions were quickly
compromised by the steady plop of poop that he subjected us
to as we sat directly behind his ever-shifting tail. He clopped
through a village road so genial that the villagers, either sipping
tea seated on small charpoys or milling around a marketplace,
called out to our group repeatedly with friendly greetings.

The stepwell had a grand entrance with ancient steps that
meandered nine stories below the ground. Historically, this was
used as a caravanserai by tired travellers, and in this landscape,
it is still possible to imagine caravans pulled by camels like
Sikander, wending a slow path past the fort in the far distance. A
young boy appeared, offering his services as our tour guide. He
walked by our side without waiting for our answer, introducing
himself as Raju or Ranjit or perhaps Ranju, swallowing his
name in a murmur as he led us down the steep stairway steadily
skipping ahead as we put one uncertain foot in front of another.
He turned back briefly to explain that he would much rather do
this than go to school and we looked at each other balefully until
we realized that it was a weekend, so we weren't collaborating
with his truancy.

Raju had a flair for the dramatic. His grimy white shirt
flapped over his unzipped shorts as he positioned himself at the
edge of the stepwell, framed by the murky green water below.
He spoke breathlessly: 'Father, son push, take son two, push,
mother push, father jump.' As the foreigners in our group stared
wide-eyed, he explained in calmer Hindi that this was a most
popular spot for suicides, with star-crossed lovers being the most
numerous. He walked us back to the top of the stepwell and

showed us where a friend of his, just last month, had dangled from a ledge and had to be helped to safety—apparently, this was a popular spot for schoolchildren to play in. He picked up a rock and dropped it into the pool from the top, encouraging us to do the same, and listen to the delayed plops, so far, far below.

In that slightly damp monsoon breeze that flitted over the stepwell as he spoke, it was easy to conjure up the beautiful women of the harem, led by the three queens, all bedecked in the aquamarines, emeralds and burnt sienna under the desert sun, coming down to this stepwell to bathe. Raju's stories were unlike the stories associated with this stepwell in tourist brochures, but infinitely more entertaining. As he spoke, an aged shepherd stopped by with his flock of sheep, artistically posing for a picture against the faraway Neemrana fort, then held out a silent palm for compensation.

As we paid Raju for our entertainment and he urged us, with great sincerity, to return again. I wondered whether he would still be there should we go back; the bright lights of the larger cities usually draw such entrepreneurial raconteurs like magnets.

The evening brought a dusky peace in which a Rajasthani troupe performed amidst the glow of Victorian lamps and ancient fiery torches doused in fuel. The sun descended into the hills as the sharp turrets blurred their edges against the darkening sky. Sitting under one of those artful chattris that curved in masonic grace to provide relief from the elements, time came to a standstill. One could imagine sinking into silks that rustled with the whiff of attar, while the heartbeat of the dhol called out to the tintinnabulating ghungroos—the dancing bells—in an ancient dance. An adult black kite wheeled overhead in concentric circles, before disappearing as a smudge into the ancient hills.

Albania is More than Mother Teresa

'Malaysian?' Our young host turned the red passport around and looked at it closely, front and back. 'We have *never* had a Malaysian tourist staying with us before!'

This would be a recurrent refrain in Albania; a mixture of awed welcome, as if Malaysians were a rare species. The first time we heard it, we had just landed in Tirana, picked up a rental car outside the modest airport named after Mother Teresa (Nënë Tereza) and driven through wild traffic to reach our small B&B, run by a Muslim family. Albania was our serendipitous find. Shqipëri or Shqipëria is what the Albanians call the Republic of Albania, a country in Southeastern Europe so long under Hoxha's closed communist regime that it was a land that time forgot. That is, until the revolutions of 1991 led to the fall of communism and the opening of the country, a country still largely undetectable on most tourist radars.

Which was a blessing for us, because Albania is, without a doubt, one of the most stunningly beautiful and hospital countries in our world.

We flew to Tirana from Barcleona, and all our costs were reduced to a fourth of Spanish prices, sometimes much lower. We expected minarets and the Azan on street corners, for this is a Muslim-majority nation (about 58 per cent of Albania's population follow Islam, making it the largest religion in the country), but decades of state atheism, which ended in 1991, meant religious practices tend to be minimal.

In this country on the Adriatic and Ionian Seas within the Mediterranean, sharing borders with Montenegro to the northwest, Kosovo to the northeast, North Macedonia to the east and Greece to the south, and there is a sense of both old and new Europe contained within Albanian shores. There are miles of European cafes dotting gorgeous shorelines, people sipping coffee at leisure, with the occasional Halal sign prominent on the footpath.

After years of being closed to the world—an Albanian tour guide described how a banana was as rare as a Coke bottle in his childhood—people of this country, no matter where you go, are intensely curious and welcoming of foreigners. Tirana, our first stop, is the capital and the largest city and driving in Tirana can be harrowing, but not impossible, for those used to the certain lawlessness of Malaysian roads. Tirana has some interesting art installations within old communist bunkers—3,000 square metres of space underground spread over several floors, this bunker was built for the elite and remained a secret for much of its existence—but the real draw of Albania is in the smaller towns.

Especially the *ancient* smaller towns, with castles perched on hilltops, where it is still affordable to book a room overnight in a castle with the Ottoman wall panelling and breathe the air that the aristocrats of the land once breathed. North of Tirana is Kruja, home of national hero Skanderbeg; there is an active market on the cobblestone streets which date to Ottoman times. Berat and Gjirokastraon, both on the UNESCO list as World Heritage sites, were unlike anything I had seen before. It forced me to stop and marvel at how things in antiquity are still clearly etched in stone and we, with our five-second reels and digital photos try to capture these ancient footprints untouched by time. Here, a permanence prevails, a slower time certainly, and also, a reminder of our own mortality.

It is easy to see why Berat is 'the town of thousand windows' as houses with big windows are piled on top of each other on a steep hillside ending in a castle. The view is especially striking from the bustling promenade filled with men playing chess in groups, or from across the river. The thirteenth-century castle, where we stayed overnight, is spectacular, within a whitewashed fortress that feels like a maze, filled with the ancient neighbourhood of homes jostling with churches and open courtyards, where the fragrance of chamomile is underfoot, and wildflowers grow untrammelled in the spaces between the old cobblestones. Some churches in this area date back to the thirteenth century, and the Red Mosque dates to the fifteenth century.

Long before I stepped on Albanian soil, I had read about Gjirokastra, a town that Ismail Kadare made famous. In *Chronicle in Stone*, Ismail Kadare's opening lines about Gjirokastra (translated by Arshi Pipa) paint the stone walls in wondrous anthropomorphic hues:

> It was a strange city, and seem to have been cast up in the valley one winter's night like some prehistoric creature that was now clawing its way up the mountain side. Everything in the city was old and made of stone, from the streets and fountains to the roofs of the sprawling age-old houses covered with grey slates like gigantic scales. It was hard to believe that, under this powerful carpace, the tender flesh of life survived and reproduced.

Over the centuries, Albania has been inhabited by different civilizations—Illyrians, Thracians, Greeks, Romans, Byzantines, Venetians, and the Ottomans—and the ruins of a stunning

Illyrian city is a day trip from Tirana. This ancient windswept city, Apollonia, is still mostly buried underground, but what blooms excavated above ground, feels like a portal elsewhere. Elegant pillars from the restored facade of the city's second-century walls tower over verdant green, among olive groves, picturesque from any angle. There is a museum complex that sheds light on the archaeological site, and inside the complex is the Byzantine monastery and Church of St Mary, which has gargoyles on the outside pillars and impressive Roman floor mosaics inside.

Butrint in The Albanian Riviera, is another ancient site worth travelling a long way to see. We drove through soaring mountainous passes, stopping only to allow donkeys to cross, sometimes to buy honey beyond the buzzing hives. We passed lakes that look like eyes of blue. The ruins of Butrint are a part of a national park and contain a variety of periods spanning 2,500 years.

Food in Albania was always wonderful, served with locally grown vegetables and fresh olive oil. At Café Kanda in Himare, we stumbled into a small family eatery, where the father fished, the mother cooked, and the son —the only one who spoke English—served with genuine delight, and it was one of the highlights of the journey. We had many extraordinary culinary experiences in Albania, and loved it all; the slow-cooked stews thick with tomatoes and cottage cheese; lamb baked into rice with yoghurt and eggs, or served grilled in a light marinade; pastries stuffed with sweet or savoury fillings. The seafood was never a disappointment.

The Albanian language is unique in Europe and has its own branch on the linguistic tree. English is widely spoken, but you will find that Albanian hospitality needs no translation. Learn this word before you go, for you will use it often and mean it from the bottom of your heart: *faleminderit—thank you.*

Finding Shambala

The light bursts through the swaying palms like a storm in the sky, diffused, molten. The morning is young, and the dew clings to a fog that hovers over fields of wheat and mustard and lentils, swirling the indistinct green to yellow and brown, then into a mass suffused with gold. At places, the fog and the sun make the open fields look like the desert of undulating dunes, then the light changes and it is just a wintry day in Gaya.

It is a walk up to the cave. Lined by beggar children and monkeys of the same size, the path appears vaguely menacing. The shopkeepers are upset when I call the animals monkeys—they are the image of Hanuman, they huff, and therefore godly. I am unconvinced but climb up the steps next to an especially populous simian family. I reach for the camera in my purse, expecting them to leap in the expectation of food, but they are calm, and some even look away. I are discomfited by these creatures, used as I am to monkeys in Southeast Asia, and once had a monkey snatch a camera away in Bali.

The cave is small—its fame made me expect something spectacular, with vaulted ceilings and elaborate frescoes like the Ajanta. Or the vibe of a Sistine Chapel. This cave seems primitive, a womblike space housing an emaciated Buddha, his ribs on display, on a path to Nirvana. On another wall are the statues of two female Indian goddesses in the requisite gold threadwork, smeared with red vermilion.

An elderly priest enters, takes some vermilion out of a packet and mimics applying a tika, so I bent forwards, forehead to his thumb. Then he offers some nuts and raisins, and when I still don't take out a purse, a piece of broken coconut. I give in, and in the dim light, search for the ten-rupee notes. I hope he'll let me just sit in a corner and meditate in the ancient cave, without asking for anything more.

The butter lamps lit outside are still burning by the time I come out. The path to the cave is not the toughest trek I've done, but it still makes me stop at a few paces, ostensibly to take pictures of the panorama unfolding below. The stray dogs are listless even though it is February and the air is cool. The children begging for alms are relentless—they follow asking for money, then bread, then even a packet of biscuits on sale at intervals through the walk up that hill and so many of them, all large eyes and small hands, all calling out *sister, auntie, didi,* anything that'll get me to stop awhile. There is a grievous vastness to their want that nothing I do now will alleviate.

In the car, I pass an arid stretch of land. It comes as a great surprise among the verdant fields, the bloom of a Japanese orange blossom tree and the greenery of pipal leaves. The driver smiles at my surprise and promises me a story.

* * *

Years ago, when Ram, Lakshman and Sita were banished to the forests for fourteen years, they stopped here, at this lake at Gaya. This old Vaishnav mandir in black marble has stood sentry for centuries for the large number of pilgrims praying for the salvation of their ancestors, for this is an ancient spot, well-favoured for *pind daan* among Hindus. A pind is a food offering in a circular form, usually made by kneading rice or barley flour, and offered to the deceased.

Dasarath, the father of Ram and Lakshman, died during his son's banishment (that too as a result of a poor man's curse, but that's another long story). Ram and Lakshman received news of their father's demise and set out to gather the things for a pind daan. They travelled far, leaving Sita at the banks of the river with a priest. As the day wore on, and evening fell, the priest started to get agitated, peering at the arc of the sun as the auspicious time faded to inauspicious night. According to the Vedas, the pind daan must be conducted at a specified time or the soul of the diseased wanders tormented, forever. As the shadows lengthened and the edges of the huts erased into the darkening sky, the agitated soul of Dasarath, sensing imminent doom, hovered over the scene. A flock of kites wheeled overhead, their shrill screeches tugging at Sita's heart.

'Is there nothing we can do Panditji?'

The Pandit looked at the woman before him and said gravely, 'There is only one thing to do. *You* must give the pind before the inauspicious time begins.'

'Me? That is impossible! My father-in-law had many sons, how can I, a mere daughter-in-law, a woman, even think of such a sin?'

'There is no alternative. If Dasarath's soul is not to be tormented in eternal hell, you must give the pind, and soon.'

And so she did.

When Ram and Lakshman returned to the river, there was an air of calm. The priest, about to depart, was stopped by the two brothers, when Sita told them that the pind daan had already been completed.

'Impossible!'

Sita explained how she had fashioned a circle of pind out of clay, mud and sand, and Dasarth's hand had risen from the waters to accept it.

'A fantastic tale indeed! How are we to believe it?' asked the brothers.

'I have five witnesses,' retorted Sita. 'Ask the river, or the priest, or ask the cow that stood there watching, or the leaves of this tree that shaded us, or this tulsi plant flourishing in the weeds . . . ask any of them!'

Ram turned to the river and asked her first. The river thought, *This God has come to my shores. Yet he hasn't even dipped his feet in my waters yet. If I speak the truth, he will leave in anger and I will never be blessed by his touch.*

So, she denied having seen anything.

Sita turned to the river in a fit of anger and cursed, 'O lying river, may you flow for all time but never be seen by the human eye.'

And so it came to pass that the Phalgu river, even today, flows below the surface of a desiccated brown silt. The pilgrims scratch at the surface with their hands to find the water flowing below, a river shrouded in invisibility even when it rains, the rainwater appearing for a day or two before disappearing below the earth again.

Ram then turned to the priest and asked him, 'O priest, do tell us the truth . . . what happened here?'

The priest looked at the two brothers and thought, *I have not been paid a coin in dakshina although this woman has completed the pind daan. Now if the brothers are told it has been done, I will surely not receive any money at all.*

So, the priest too denied the pind daan.

And Sita turned to the priest and cursed him, 'O vile priest, no matter how much your kind gets paid, your lust for money will always make you unhappy. You will never live a life that is fulfilled!' And so it has been with priests since then.

Then the brothers turned to the tulsi plant and asked her for the truth.

The Tulsi plant also thought, *Here is Ram, a God. He will use me in the pind daan and that will be my salvation. If I say the pind has been done, he may even curse me anger, especially as the river and the priest will make me look like a liar.*

So the tulsi plant also denied the pind daan.

And Sita cursed the Tulsi, 'O Tulsi, though you will remain holy, you will be always worshipped outside the home, never invited inside.'

And so it has been, for all time.

When the brothers asked the cow about what had happened, the cow thought, *Look at all the flowers and food the brothers have returned with! I got nothing to eat from Sita's pind daan, but if the brothers give the pind now, all the edibles will come to me.*

And she denied the pind daan.

And Sita cursed her with, 'O cow-mother, although you will still be holy, our rituals will only use the unclean backside of yours and not the front.'

And so it has been, that gomutra (cow urine) and gomaya (cow dung) is required in rituals.

Finally, the brothers turned to the tree. 'O tree, four of the witnesses have spoken their truth. What is yours?'

And the tree, with nothing to lose and with no feelings of greed or personal gain, spoke the truth. It described how Sita had given the pind daan as the evening had begun to descend and how Dasarath's hand had reached out from the waters to accept it.

Today, the tree flourishes everywhere. Sita was vindicated, although this would not be the last time that her husband would not take her at her word.

* * *

One of the nicest perks of being a writer is that it is a great excuse to travel, all in the guise of research. Although Shambala Junction is an imaginary place, writing the novel titled *Shambala Junction* took me on lovely long train journeys through India.

Shambala Junction begins with a rather jinxed train journey for the protagonist, Iris, an Indian-American young woman visiting India with her new fiancée. I mined the memories of my own childhood, especially the wonderful nostalgia of long train journeys from New Delhi Station to Howrah in Kolkata, to write Iris's wide-eyed enchantment with the ubiquitous details of Indian life.

Every summer, when the heat drove Delhiites to cooler cities, my family would board the Rajdhani Express, for a twenty-four-hour journey with a long halt at Mughal Serai. Mughal Serai was a magical place in my childhood, with makeshift stalls frying fresh food and craftsmen selling colourful wooden dolls. It is impossible to find these artisanal wooden toys at railway stations any more but Aman's stall is inspired by my vivid memories:

> He had an array of colourful wooden dolls spread out in front of him on a pushcart: there were dolls with turbans and flared coats playing flutes and dholaks; there were men riding horses with colourful stirrups and dazzling sword-sheaths; there were dancers dancing with the left leg slightly on tiptoe, caught in mid-swirl in the disarray of flouncing skirts.

I started writing this novel after being enraged at the tone of an article about 'baby shopping' which was about international adoptions fuelling child trafficking in India. This is a global problem, not just limited to India, and the trafficking moves from one impoverished country to another as the authorities start clamping down on severe irregularities. I wanted the world to realize that we are all complicit in this, especially by pretending that if poor children are placed in affluent homes it makes the world a better place. But surely there are many ways to improve the future of impoverished children without transplanting them out of familiar places where they are surrounded by loved ones, especially as most are taken at an age when they are unable to articulate a preference? The cost of doing good should not be based on a geography of entitlement, where adopted children prosper in new Western homes, leaving their natal homes fractured in the process.

I wrote the first draft in about three months in Amsterdam, then I edited this novel over four years, toning down the rage, for this novel taught me that it was more than an easy fable about the consumerist north versus the impoverished south of the globe, and needed nuanced characters. I became aware of how easy it was for me, as an author, to climb on to soapboxes.

This story shifted, from being based in Delhi, to an imaginary Shambala Junction, loosely based on Gaya. Gaya is an ancient city and a deeply spiritual place where the Buddha attained enlightenment. It has a real hill where the Buddha preached the Fire Sermon and a Mahabodhi temple, and these feature in the novel as well. At the same time, Gaya is also within the state of Bihar, which was at that time considered one of the most badly governed, lawless and corrupt states in India. I travelled to Gaya alone to get a sense of the place and visited the Mahabodhi temple, with its most international gathering of Buddhist pilgrims from all around the world alongside tourists like me. I visited the cave with the emaciated Buddha figure—an image rarely portrayed in Buddhist iconography—a startling image, a reminder of the frailty of all human conditions.

The hill where Buddha preached the Fire Sermon was a hike, and in the novel, I transmute my experience into the voice of Emily, a Canadian woman wanting to adopt an Indian girl-child:

> Emily raised her head. She could see the motley group of children heading for the next tourist bus pulling in. They had no time for play; it was work for them as long as tourists like her showed up. She felt her eyes prickle; so many children with miserable lives. Too many children who could not be adopted into better lives.
>
> Beside a square white enclosure it was all brown on the hill. The rough-hewn rocks scattered on the dusty ground made room for brown shoots to limply wave in the wind. Her skin tingled with a tragic epiphany; on this hill, pregnant with religious history, she could see absolutely no signs of life.

Unlike Emily, my trip to Gaya left me with a very happy memory. During my visit to the Mahabodhi temple, as I sat under the Bodhi tree meditating with other people at the site where the Buddha had attained Nirvana, a stray leaf twirled down from the green canopy of the Bodhi Pallanka overhead and fell into my lap. That dried leaf is now framed and hangs in my home in Chicago; I like to think that the Buddha approved this story much before it found a publisher or won a prize.

Never a Lovely So Real

I give you Chicago. It is not London and Harvard. It is not Paris and buttermilk. It is American in every chitling and sparerib. It is alive from snout to tail.

—H. L. Mencken

When I arrived in Chicago in 2012, fresh from a Shanghai that pulsated like the centre of the universe, I expected a boring midwestern city with pretensions—like the giant lake shoring the city—of being an ocean of greatness. Nobody spoke of Chicago with the breathlessness of New York or Paris, or even Amsterdam.

But Chicago surprised me. In Printers Row, where I now live, I discovered an antiquarian bookshop, red-bricked from 1896, that had an ancient copy of *The Rime of the Ancient Mariner*, old broadsides and a Bollywood seventies heroine as the screensaver. It seemed to encompass the literary world—embrace my complicated global influences—and I fell in love.

> *Printers Row, Chicago*
> *I come to Chicago*
> *resisting assimilation.*
>
> *From old cities in Europe*
> *to the older ruins of Asia,*

I have resisted the hyphenations
the identity reconstructions,
of tired–huddled–masses,
in this adulterated corner
of the globe.

Until, in Printer's Row
—in an antiquarian bookshop,
red-bricked from 1896—
a man reads from the distressed
first edition of the Rime, hardcover
separated from spine, stark lines drawn
above an idle ship on a painted ocean;
He knows Tagore, and on his desktop
is the image of Waheeda,
incandescent beauty.

He talks about translators,
epics, New York broadsides;
In that tiny shop, laying bare the
nuances—the proclivity of
imagination—of this brave new world

Printers Row is named after the flourishing trade in books that had its heart here. The M.A. Donohue & Co. Building still stands at Plymouth Court and Polk Street, and if you walk past the Franklin Building, look up to see the stunning tiles of printing tradesmen such as a bookbinder and typesetter as well as a painted tile mural of the Gutenberg Bible.

There is the independent bookstore, Sandmeyers, next to a park where concrete reproductions of printer blocks function as seating. There is a model of a life-sized printing press in another corner. Everywhere you turn, there is the Word, immortalized through time, in brick and cement and art.

In short, this city is a bibliophile's paradise. I felt I was living within the shelf of a beloved library, every book within reach.

> Come and show me another city with lifted head singing so proud to be alive and coarse and strong and cunning . . . proud to be Hog Butcher, Tool Maker, Stacker of Wheat, Player with Railroads and Freight Handler to the Nation.
>
> —Carl Sandburg

Approximately fifteen kilometres away from my home in Chicago is the Ernest Hemingway's Birthplace Museum, where this Nobel laureate was born on 21 July 1899. Hemingway modelled an uncompromising masculinity in twentieth-century prose.

In this leafy upscale suburb, flanked by homes designed by architect Frank Lloyd Wright, this stately birthplace of Hemingway is a Queen Anne building with a turret and wraparound porch, now lovingly restored. Visitors are ushered into the parlour, which has been recreated from photographs left by Dr Hemingway, Ernest's father, and the descriptions left in the writing of Ernest's sister Marcelline. The rose on the cornices matches the wallpaper exactly, and dappled sunlight falls on a writing desk, cluttered with books from that era.

Hemingway was born in a second-floor bedroom of this home of his maternal grandparents, and spent the first six years of his life with his Grandfather Abba, teller of tales and hater of war. His father, Dr Clarence Edmonds Hemingway, was a physician, and presided over the births of all his six children. Ernest's mother, Grace, was a remarkable woman. Despite the constraints of her time, she had moved to New York to pursue a musical career and was a well-respected artiste who out-earned her physician husband.

This is a home filled with music and books and light streaming through the ancient trees. Years later, Dr Hemingway would die by suicide with a shotgun, and Ernest Hemingway would end his own life at the age of 61 in a similar manner. Ernest would lose two of his siblings to suicide, and his daughter, Gloria, would be found dead in 2001 as a transwoman, under very suspicious circumstances.

Hemingway would marry four times, write sparse prose on war and bullfighting which Virginia Woolf would describe as 'self-consciously virile'. He would build a cult of performative masculinity that writers like me find virulently misogynistic.

In this house—Ernest's home until he was six years of age— frames the image of a gentle boy, his crib placed close enough to his sister Marcelline's, so they could hold hands through the bars at night.

There is also the picture of Ernest, as a one-year-old, dressed in frilly lace outfit.

Following the fashion of the times, Ernest's mother was determined to present her two eldest children as twin girls. Ernest, younger than Marcelline by eighteen months, was dressed as a girl until he was at least five years old; Marcelline was held back in school by their mother so that the impression of twinhood could persist.

It is a matter of speculation, of course, how much of Ernest's later hyper-masculinity was a rebellion against his mother, whom he hated and blamed for his father's suicide.

Themes of women and death would recur in his work. Emasculation is also notable in Hemingway's work, in *God Rest You Merry, Gentlemen* and *The Sun Also Rises*. Hemingway would label his writing style the iceberg theory, a spare and lean narrative prose that relied on the theory of omission, and was in sharp contrast to the more flowery literary English of the times.

There is no doubt that he changed the nature of American writing, and moulded the language of the short story. He brought a sense of peripatetic travel (used bilingual puns and codeswitched sentences), and nurtured a braggadocio and machismo seen as misogynistic, homophobic and racist. *Hills Like White Elephants*, a short story by Ernest Hemingway, first published in August 1927, is a masterclass in dialogue-writing, and I have used it with students in Kuala Lumpur, Chicago, New Delhi and Amsterdam, for the terse prose cuts across global lines.

In this home in Oak Park, filled with family memorabilia and photographs, is a poignant reminder of the early years of Ernest Hemingway. He was born into an elite family which revered learning, words, painting, music and modern gadgets, but also a family of contradictions and personal tragedies.

'You can't get away from yourself by moving from one place to another', wrote Hemingway, in *The Sun Also Rises*.

Chicago is a city of writers.

> Yet once you've come to be part of this particular patch, you'll never love another. Like loving a woman with a broken nose, you may well find lovelier lovelies. But never a lovely so real.
>
> —Nelson Algren

Chicago is a city often compared to a war zone, with drive-by shootings and violent robberies, and recently, downtown looting that left shopfronts boarded up for months.

I live next to the iconic Harold Washington Public Library. Every morning, I pass five massive owls looking down at me; four twelve-foot high owls stand at the corners of the roof and a fifth great horned owl is on top of the main entrance of the building on State Street. The fifth owl is twenty-foot high with a twenty-foot wingspan and weighs three tonnes, and it clutches an open book with wings spread, ready to take flight. The owls are augmented with swirls of leaves and seed pods, representing growth and wisdom, but the effect is of the owls on fire, aggressively positioned. Even as their one foot clutches loose papers, the other has talons raised, ready to strike.

I love spending time at this library with a beautiful Winter Garden on the top floor, open to all the citizens of this city. It provides refuge to the homeless, classes for the marginalized, and wisdom for borrowing. Yet this space, too, is often fraught with a contained sense of violence:

Public Library, Computer Commons

Young girl, child hidden inside pram. Whimpers
sound through silence, shredding clucks to screaming,
JUST SHUT UP! SHUT THE FUCK UP'; baby shrieks
louder. I'm up, to grab my printout, purse
in hand. See man in voluminous black reach
out, but not fast enough. The security guard
takes my open backpack, files spilling out,
Mac yawning, still half closed. Guard glares Fuckwit
look, says 'Things disappear here.' Behind,
two men trade Spanglish fighting words, gestures.
I lean against the wall to zip my bags
when a teen slides smoothly in my seat
and turns the screen as if I'm invisible.

In cities buzzing foreign tongues—where words
repose in fogs of sound, the pronouns merging
into nouns and verbs indistinct—it takes
the ear three months to parse phonemes. But here,
in Chicago, reined-in violence translates
to fiery noise, devoid of the syntax

of civility. A rage, unquiet, paces
dark shelves of accumulated wisdom,
like wolves—slavering, lean, uninvited—
outside the reaches of feast and light.

A few blocks away from this most postmodern edifice, is the old library, now the Chicago Cultural Center. The Chicago Cultural Center faces the Millennium Park and overlooks the iconic Bean sculpture by Anish Kapoor, and is now a venue for the performing, visual and literary arts. Every year, I spent the whole night at the annual *Ragamala*, under the magnificent Tiffany dome of the Preston Bradley Hall, listening to live Indian classical music. Around the dome is inscribed 'Books are the legacies that a great genius leaves to humankind, which are delivered down from generation to generation'.

The concert ends at dawn, with a morning raga; the sun breaks through the cold Chicago dark as exquisite sitar and tablas play in tandem, ending twelve hours of musical transcendence. in a magnificent finale. It is one of my absolute favourite events in Chicago, wedding words and music and performance. I find my breath thrumming to the sounds from my childhood, my heart beating in rhythm.

I am an organic Chicagoan. Living there has given me a multiplicity of characters to aspire for. I hope to live there the rest of my days.

—Gwendolyn Brooks

The American Writers Museum is on Michigan Avenue, a few blocks away from me, and offers a cornucopia of programming, as does the Poetry Foundation. My doorman is an avid reader, and we talk books. There is so much happening with literary activities, that one is spoilt for choice. The bar in my neighbourhood is named The First Draft, and the closest bookstore to me is Exile in Booksville . . . there is wordplay everywhere.

I came to Chicago reluctantly, expecting to stay for three years. It has been 12 years already, and I don't plan to leave.

You wake up in Chicago, pull back the curtain, and you KNOW where you are. You could be nowhere else. You are in a big, brash, muscular, broad shouldered motherfuckin' city. A metropolis, completely non-neurotic, ever-moving, big hearted but cold blooded machine with millions of moving parts—a beast that will, if disrespected or not taken seriously, roll over you without remorse. It is, also, as I like to point out frequently, one of America's last great NO BULLSHIT zones. Pomposity, pretentiousness, putting on airs of any kind, douchery and lack of a sense of humor will not get you far in Chicago . . . Chicago is a town, a city that doesn't ever have to measure itself against any other city. Other places have to measure themselves against it. It's big, it's outgoing, it's tough, it's opinionated, and everybody's got a story.

—Anthony Bourdain

A Light in the Dark

My father is ninety-three-years-old. His memory fails him. 'Eat,' Papa urges, reaching into a tin of biscuits and foraging for the type I like best. 'Eat, Ma, dunk this one into your tea.' He extends a round Marie biscuit, and I am five years old again.

It is the fifth biscuit he has handed me this morning, but I take it from his gnarled yet steady fingers. His offering of food and my acceptance of it is the vocabulary of love.

I have flown 7,500 miles from Chicago, where I have lived for the past eleven years. I left my home in Delhi over three decades ago, and have worked in many parts of the world, but the US, where I came to study for a doctoral degree, has become home.

Now, I am in Delhi again, for Bhai Phota.

I have not missed Bhai Phota for the past five years, not since Amit, the eldest of my three brothers, suffered a traumatic brain injury after a bicycling accident in 2016.

I am the only sister, the only one who can perform the ritual that ensures the longevity of my brothers, and after Amit's accident, Bhai Phota's protective rite has been non-negotiable for me. Even during the pandemic, when the journey required multiple COVID tests and a week-long quarantine in a separate apartment, it was important not to miss this.

Whenever I call from Chicago, Papa asks, 'When are you coming again?' Watching my biscuit dissolve into the tea,

I know this will be one of the last meals I share with my father. But even more than for him and my eighty-three-year-old mother, I have come to Delhi for my brothers.

* * *

My childhood was filled with stories from *Thakumar Jhuli*, a wildly popular collection of Bengali folklore by Dakshinaranjan Mitra Majumdar that was first published in 1907. My favourite story features Kiranmala, a princess who undertakes a long and dangerous journey to find her missing brothers Arun and Barun, both of whom have been petrified into stone by an evil spell. When she reaches the site where her brothers lie enchanted, she sprinkles magic waters on the rocks, transforming them into people—including the two petrified princes.

I grew up believing a sister's love can bring back to consciousness that which lies inert.

So, while I am in Delhi, I read to Amit every day. He is under round-the-clock care from a skilled nursing staff. When he sees me, he raises a thumb to say yes or a forefinger to say no. That is his only mode of communication.

Before the accident, he had one of the finest brains in the country. He was a professor of computer science at the Indian Institute of Technology Kanpur. After the accident, the best neurologists and neurosurgeons of Delhi, Mumbai and Chennai all rallied to save his precious brain. *Pray for a miracle*, Amit's neurosurgeon had advised.

Every year, especially at Bhai Phota, I do just that.

* * *

Papa is sprightly as we walk out to the balcony, where the golden light of the sun is sieved through the leaves of the mango tree that shaded my girlhood. When my father bought this plot of land, it was in an undesirable part of Delhi, where wolves bayed at night, called the East Pakistan Displaced Persons (EPDP) Colony. His family had abandoned their ancestral home in what is now Bangladesh following the Partition of India; his widowed mother faced a life of penury in newly independent India, with seven children to feed, and he left home at fourteen to make a living.

A pejorative term, EPDP differentiated the wretched refuse of the partition from the families who had lived in Delhi for generations. Now, this area is named Chittaranjan Park, and it falls within upscale South Delhi. Yet Chittaranjan Park remains at heart a Bengali para, a communal enclave where we know our neighbours, and Bengali is the default language of the shopkeepers.

My other elder brother, Sumit, lives with his family just three houses away. My younger brother, Atish, lives in Boston with his young family, and he is unable to come. Sumit was a Colonel in the Indian Army and retired from the armed forces to take up a corporate job with one of India's leading tech firms. Soon after Amit's accident, Sumit resigned from his corporate position as the medical situation at home, with Amit and my ageing parents, grew in complexity. Unlike his diasporic siblings, Sumit is always there, for festivals and emergencies alike.

Sumit joins us on the porch as we bask in the gentle light; despite the pollution and the smog, the wintry sunshine is magic. It carries the heft of years of sitting on charpoys, breaking hot peanut shells with our teeth and sipping on hot chai; the fragrance of kochuri made with tender winter peas and spiced potatoes eaten on an open balcony, just as we are doing today. Fat crows flit from the ancient bel tree to the sajna, old childhood friends.

Sumit and I discuss the menu for Bhai Phota. In our family, it is always beer and biryani; the only thing we have to decide is where to order the food from. Hindutva politics, which has grown increasingly fanatical, seeks to enforce vegetarianism as the default way to celebrate Hinduism, but that movement is steeped in North Indian traditions, foreign to Bengalis. We refuse to compromise on Paet Puja (literally translated as the worship of the stomach) as an equally important way to honour our heritage. We decide on the Kolkata lamb biriyani—with chunks of potato and boiled egg—and chicken kebabs on the side.

Papa approves of our menu decisions. He still enjoys his beer; at his age, it is available so rarely.

* * *

This is how our festival calendar unfolds: First comes Chotti Diwali, Little Diwali. For Bengalis, Chotti Diwali is also Bhoot Chaturdashi, when the benign fourteen generations of ancestor spirits roam the earth. We light fourteen lamps at the corners of our homes, illuminating dark nooks and crannies to attract ancestral blessings. The next night is Diwali when all homes in Delhi blaze with lights. On Diwali night, Bengalis also celebrate Kali Puja, chanting prayers to the Goddess Kali throughout the night. Then, two days after Diwali night, in the morning, we have Bhai Phota, to celebrate our bond with our siblings.

Diwali is a week away when Tinni, Sumit's twenty-four-year-old daughter and the only granddaughter of our clan, joins me in attending an open-air weekend craft bazaar at the Sunder Nursery, a heritage garden complex. Tinni is never far from the family Labrador, Bhombol Bumble, who also tags along.

This year, we expect the festivities to be less boisterous, as more people are staying within their homes, but on Diwali all houses must blaze with lights so that the Goddess of plenty, Lakshmi, finds her path clearly lit. So we're at the bazaar to buy diyas, traditional terra-cotta lamps that are fragile but flicker all night with the prettiest of lights. Bhombol ignores us as we shop, eating whatever is proffered and falling into a satiated sleep at the stall that sells canine treats.

The Sunder Nursery complex is an archaeological site, flanked by the stunning Humayun's Tomb and the historic Purana Qila. The old coexists with the new; amid modern greenhouses are scattered the remains of Mughal structures, the names tripping off my tongue like poetry—Lakkarwala Burj, Sunder Burj, Sunderwala Mahal. We pause to admire the curlicues of Quranic inscriptions. Sandstone lattice screens, open to the wintry sun, light our way.

We explore as much as we can but the grounds—all seventy acres—are too expansive to cover entirely. The Archaeological Society of India has teamed up with the Aga Khan Trust for Culture to beautifully restore and preserve the site. When earthworks revealed a sixteenth-century lotus pond that would have stood within the garden of the Sunder Burj and Sunderwala Mahal, they rebuilt it so that the lotuses once again bloom in the pond outside. Inside, on the ornamental domed ceiling, vivid depictions of red and blue flowers burst from the stonework. The sight takes our breath away.

* * *

The day before Diwali, the streets are a riot of colour from garlands of flowers, brightly painted religious figurines, colourful sweets, and handcarts teetering with plump seasonal fruits. In the Bengali fish markets, rows of sweet river fish—

ilish and rui and papda—jostle the pomfret and glistening king prawns. This is the time for feasting.

I make a last dash for artisanal diyas, at Project WHY, which sells the lamps to support its mission to educate and feed street children in Delhi. The intrepid teachers are back to educate the children in groups of five at a time, so that they can keep learning—and having a daily meal—despite coming from homes where internet connections and computers are an impossibility. The diyas the teachers make are artistic and cheerful—blues and yellows and reds and greens and purples merge with shiny sequins and glitter, and everything is heaped delightfully on bright trays like confectionery. It's hard to stop buying.

Back home, as evening comes, we dress in saris and light fourteen lamps around the house. I light five lamps outside Amit's bedroom, one for every year since the accident, inviting the ancestral spirits to come and spread the light.

On Diwali night, the city switches on all its lights. Even the Sikh gurdwaras and Muslim mosques are festooned with twinkling fairy lights. Flower-patterned rangolis adorn the outsides of homes, and Bengali porches welcome visitors with white alpona designs, motifs of flowers and animals and geometric patterns drawn with rice flour that will feed ants for days to come.

The sonorous conch shell and ringing bells of the Kali Puja issue from the main Kali temple in Chittaranjan Park all night. The temple rises from a hill in a blaze of lights, a huge white lotus flower incandescent at the entrance. The roof shines red and yellow and the beautiful terracotta friezes on the walls glow, illuminating dancing Gods and cavorting lovers and grazing cattle—a world where there is peace and beauty at every turn.

* * *

My mother wakes me early on Bhai Phota morning to make preparations. There is the dhan-durbo (trident-shaped grass and unhusked rice) to be gathered, the bell metal tray and the copper lamp to be polished. Tinni arranges sweets around the lamp, fits in the dhan-durbo. I hold a mango leaf smeared with ghee over an open flame, and the fire makes a smoky kaajal, a traditional kohl. We grind sandalwood paste and collect it into a tiny stone bowl, and smear vermilion paste on another leaf.

Why has Bhai Phota brought me back to Delhi every year, to chant a mantra and put a mark of kaajal-sandalwood-vermilion on my brothers' foreheads? I understand that words don't confer immortality—although, as a writer, I know of nothing else that so effectively does—but I choose to believe that there is magic in the brass lamplight, the smoky blackness from ghee on the underside of a mango leaf, the pastes we grind, the flowers plucked fresh, and the auspicious grass and grain.

Most of all, there is magic in the unwavering love that makes us all come together to pray for wellness, if not immortality. Our mantras may be in mere words, but in their sonorous repetition is the hope of averting any misfortune for our loved one.

The six of us dress in new clothes, except for Bumble Bhombol, (whom Papa has to shoo away from the plates of food). Amit gives a big thumbs-up when he sees us all milling around. I give a phota to Amit, then one to Sumit, and there is much levity as my parents argue about the words in the mantra, and I forget the order of the lines. Papa gets a phota from Tinni, then Bhombol gets one too.

I feed my brothers sweets from the prayer tray, to sweeten their lives. I am careful to feed Amit only a smidgen, for he chokes easily. I dip a finger into my beer and place a drop on his tongue. He swallows.

The biryani follows, the recipe dating to when the Nawab of Awadh was dethroned in the nineteenth century and poverty forced the cook to add eggs and potatoes to biryani meat and rice. Lovers of Hyderabadi and Lucknow biryani shudder at the blasphemy of potatoes in any biryani, but Kolkata biryani is sublime, and we eat every last bit.

Our celebration is communal, for Bhai Phota embraces kin that are not related by blood, and although the pandemic keeps our gathering small, I address everyone as Bhaiya, my brother: the male nurses who look after Amit night and day, the attendants who help them, the house helpers who look after my parents. We feast on the savoury and finish with three kinds of sweets, including a yoghurt, mishti doi, sweetened with a rare palm jaggery that's only available in winter.

I soak in every minute with my family—especially with Sumit. I see how he manages the delicate ballet of staying upbeat in the face of a tragedy that he can't fly away from, ever. The miracle is in the depth of our love for each other, for our parents, and for Amit. We squeeze each other tight, not letting go. Being able to do this, in this year of losses and heartbreaks, makes this holiday all the more precious.

Acknowledgement

I am grateful for the time of many people who appear in these pages, in so many parts of the world. Thank you for stopping to speak and share your stories with me.

The Penguin Random House SEA team—Nora Nazerene Abu Bakar, Amberdawn Manaois—thank you for midwifing this book into being, and for the publicity team of Pallavi Narayan, Garima Bhatt and Chaitanya Srivastava for telling the world about this. For a most excellent book cover, I have the talented Vibha Surya to thank.

Gratitude also to Diana Khoo of *The Edge, Malaysia* who commissioned many of these essays and gave a column to express myself in; to *World Literature Today*'s most excellent editors, Michelle M. Johnson and Daniel A. Simon, who have published much of my work; and the most excellent editors at *Hemispheres, Newsweek, Los Angeles Review of Books, Scroll India, Verge, Muse India,* and *Poetry Foundation,* among others, who took my raw words and improved them substantially for publication.

Bettina Chua Abdullah not only runs the Fay Khoo Book Award in Malaysia to honour Malaysian Food writing, she honoured *Paet Puja* with an award, then became a beta reader for this collection. A distinguished writer herself, she vastly improved this manuscript with her feedback, and I couldn't be more grateful. Also grateful to my readers in Chicago, Rachel

Swearingen and Natalia Nebel, for editorial fixes and their unflagging cheerleading.

A DCASE award from the City of Chicago enabled me to have the time as resources to work on this book and submit it for publication, and included an inspirational time at Xochi Quetzal in Chapala, Mexico in 2022. A Ragdale Fellowship, a Sacatar Foundation Fellowship, and Rimbun Dahan's Southeast Asian Arts Residency in Malaysia, as well as my time as Scholar-in-Residence at the International Institute of Asian Studies in Leiden, the Netherlands, contributed vastly to this collection.

This is a book about finding a home in the world. Home has always been where my parents have been, even if the landscape outside was always shifting, and for that skill of making a home anywhere, I thank my parents, Kalidas and Pratima Mukherjee. This book also attests to the unflagging support of my brothers, Amit Mukherjee, Ashis Mukherjee and Atish Mukherjee, and my extended family around the world. I feel blessed indeed.

As an adult, it has been Prasanta Dutt, Arohan Dutt and Arush Dutt, who have been the centre of my nomadic compass. Especially Prasanta . . . home is, without a doubt, wherever in the world you are.

Publication Credits

'Singing of Coronavirus' (formerly titled 'Singing of Covid through an Ancient Art Form: The Patuas of Bengal') was first published in *World Literature Today*, October 2022.

'Albania is More than Mother Teresa' (formerly titled 'Why Albania is more than just its links with modern-day saint Mother Teresa') was first published in *The Edge*, on July 30, 2022.

'A Light in the Dark' first appeared in *Hemispheres*. November 2021.

'Through the Lens of Danish Siddiqui' (formerly titled 'Through the Lens of Courage and Humanity: A Tribute to Danish Siddiqui') was first published in *The Edge*, on July 23, 2021.

'Tears and Song', Pandemic Dispatches first appeared in *World Literature Today*, June 18, 2021.

'To Keep My Brother Alive, I Will Fly 7,500 Miles for Diwali' first appeared in *Los Angeles Review of Books* on May 6, 2021.

'Terrorism Finds No Room Here' was first published in *Newsweek* on 29 May, 2021.

'Hope and Mangroves' was first published by *Orion*, Winter, on December 2, 2020.

'Sudah makan?' was first published in *The Edge*, November 11, 2019.

'The Voluptuousness of Memory' first appeared in *The Edge*, July 29, 2019.

'Beacons of Inspiration' first appeared in *The Edge*, on April 29, 2019.

'Glocal Voices' (formerly titled 'Malaysian English Writing Today') was first published by *World Literature Today*, on April 16, 2019.

'Paet Puja' (formerly titled 'Paet-Puja: How Bengalis Worship the Stomach') won the 2018 Fay Khoo Award for Food+Drink Writing, Malaysia in November 2018 and was first published in *Telltale Food*, Hikayat, 2020.

'Misogyny in Bengali Nursery Rhymes' (formerly titled 'Why are many Bengali rhymes and songs for children, loved by generations, so misogynistic') appeared in *Scroll India* in September 2018.

'Do My Poems Cry with Me?' *World Literature Today*, January 2015.

'A Journey to the Dalai Lama'. *Chicago Literati*, Wanderlust Issue, August 2014.

'A Messiah in Malaysia', *Chicken Soup For the Romantic Indian Soul*, Westland Books, India. 146. 2010.

'Fortress, Feathers & Fabled waters' *Muse India*, Indian Travel Writing. Issue 25, May-June 2009.